THE POPULAR GUIDE
TO PUPPY-REARING

THE
POPULAR GUIDE
TO PUPPY-REARING

Olwen Gwynne-Jones

ELEVENTH EDITION

POPULAR DOGS

London Melbourne Sydney Auckland Johannesburg

Popular Dogs Publishing Co. Ltd

An imprint of the Hutchinson Publishing Group

17–21 Conway Street, London WIP 6JD

Hutchinson Group (Australia) Pty Ltd
30–32 Cremorne Street, Richmond South, Victoria 3121
PO Box 151, Broadway, New South Wales 2007

Hutchinson Group (NZ) Ltd
32–34 View Road, PO Box 40-086, Glenfield, Auckland 10

Hutchinson Group (SA) (Pty) Ltd
PO Box 337, Bergvlei 2012, South Africa

First published 1951
Second edition, revised 1955
Third edition 1956
Fourth edition, revised 1959
Fifth edition, revised 1961
Sixth edition, revised 1964
Seventh edition, revised 1968
Eighth edition, revised 1971
Ninth edition, revised 1973
Tenth edition 1977
Eleventh edition, revised 1981

Printed in Great Britain by The Anchor Press Ltd
and bound by Wm Brendon & Son Ltd
both of Tiptree, Essex

ISBN 0 09 143701 6

Dedicated with gratitude, to
F. ANDREW EDGSON, M.R.C.V.S.
at whose suggestion this book was written

CONTENTS

ILLUSTRATIONS

AUTHOR'S INTRODUCTION

I THINK all will agree that, in comparison with the flood of literature available on human infant welfare, there has been little written on the subject where animals are concerned. This, of course, is natural, but it does seem to me that as the adult dog is so greatly influenced by its rearing, environment, breeding and care during the first year or eighteen months of its life (and, indeed, pre-natally) a book on puppies might be useful. It is a subject which all-too-often receives scant attention and yet it is such a vitally important one. Nothing can replace actual experience learnt through the course of years, but it does seem to me rather unfortunate for our youngsters that they should suffer from our experiments and mistakes. We have all made both! But it is impossible to rear many litters of puppies throughout a long period of years without profiting by experience. I have often marvelled at the extraordinary (and may I say, peculiar!) views that breeders have on this controversial question. My own methods of rearing puppies have at least been tried and tested through the years, and judging by the hundreds of letters I have received asking for advice, they have been equally successful with puppies other than my own. I hope the new breeder will find this book helpful and, as we are never too old to learn, the old breeder may also find something to interest him in these pages.

O. G.-J.

1951

AUTHOR'S NOTES

to the Fourth Edition

IT IS naturally a great pleasure to me that a fourth edition of this little book is now required. I have had letters about it from all over the world and if I have been able, in the smallest measure, to help others in their puppy-rearing problems, I have been well rewarded. Although the basic problems remain the same, there has been a number of changes in veterinary medicine and this is reflected in additions to the text. My veterinary surgeon was kind enough to read through the revisions and also to make various suggestions, which have been incorporated. I wish to express my gratitude to him for his continued interest in this book.

1959   O. G.-J.

to the Sixth Edition

I THINK this little book has fulfilled its purpose in helping the new breeder in the fascinating tasks of rearing puppies. It seemed to me that there was a need for such a book, and I well remember that when I started breeding in 1936 I looked in vain for a book of this type. It has made the writer many friends and I believe that it has found its way into veterinary libraries as well as city libraries. Since the book was first written, veterinary science has marched ahead, especially with regard to immunisation, and these recent discoveries have been incorporated here. For comments on these and other veterinary matters I owe my veterinary surgeon, Mr. Andrew Edgson, a big debt of gratitude.

1964   O. G.-J.

to the Seventh Edition

WHEN I first wrote this book, I never imagined that it would still be in print seventeen years later. I think this demonstrates, if nothing else could, what need there was for such a book, and it is indeed a pleasure to me that it is still valued.

Various revisions have been made in the text where necessary, particularly in the constantly changing field of veterinary matters—and once again my kind and indefatigable veterinary surgeon has given his precious time to reading through the book and to making various suggestions for which I am most grateful.

1968   O. G.-J.

to the Eighth Edition

MR. ANDREW EDGSON has again made a few minor corrections to keep the veterinary information up to date in this edition.

1971   O. G.-J.

to the Ninth Edition

I AM delighted that yet another edition of *The Popular Guide to Puppy-rearing* has proved necessary. Some revisions have been made where and when necessary but the puppy-rearing methods have stood the test of time and remain unaltered. Mr. Edgson has again come to my rescue in making any necessary veterinary revisions and I am very grateful to him for his continued interest in this book.

1973   O. G.-J.

to the Tenth Edition

ON re-reading this book towards the end of 1976 I have found virtually nothing that requires revision—apart from the list of Kennel Club fees which has been brought up to date for the Addendum. It is a source of great pleasure to me that after so many years the book is still so topical and still fulfilling a need.

1977   O. G.-J.

to the Eleventh Edition

FOR this edition I have brought up-to-date the Kennel Club list of fees in the Addendum. I have also added a section on Parvovirus to the Addendum on page 98.

1981   O. G.-J.

CHAPTER I

BEFORE THE PUPPY IS BORN: CHOICE OF BROOD BITCH

I WONDER if everyone realises that the rearing of a puppy begins long before birth? Indeed, it is true to say that the future welfare of the puppy is, in some respects, decided even before the prospective mother is mated.

Let us suppose that our new breeder has acquired, from a good kennel of his breed, a nice, typical bitch, well-bred, and a suitable foundation for his new kennel. Apart from possible show points, health and temperament should be important considerations; a nervy, highly strung bitch should be avoided, and she should be in perfect health and condition.

Some forms of skin trouble are congenital or hereditary, and there are other easily transmitted defects, such as ingrowing eyelashes, and mouths either over-or undershot, which should be avoided. Whether the bitch is an adult or a youngster, the owner will be looking forward to the time when she comes in season, and when he can really feel he is on the way to becoming a fully fledged breeder.

From personal experience, I would suggest that, if finances permit, the bitch should be bought outright from the kennel, and not on what are called "breeding terms". The latter mean that, in return for paying a lower initial sum for the bitch, the owner will have to give up two or more puppies from the bitch's first (and often second) litter as part of the purchase price. Often a free stud service is given by the previous owner as an additional attraction. The bitch does not become the official property of the new owner until the conditions have been fulfilled. The flaw lies, of course, in the puppies which must be surrendered. One's first litter is (or should be) a great thrill, and having to part with what sometimes amounts to half the litter, is rather a blow, especially as the previous owner usually selects the most promising puppies. The new owner is, therefore, left with the worst of the litter (from the show point of view) or sometimes no puppies at all if the litter is a small one. The puppies must be reared by the new owner for the original owner, and if puppies from more than one litter must be surrendered, it may be years before the owner can really feel the bitch is his. It is, therefore, wise to study the conditions, and think the matter over very carefully before buying a bitch on breeding terms.

Before breeding from a bitch, it is necessary to register her at the Kennel Club, 1–4 Clarges Street, London, W.1, from which the appropriate forms may be obtained.[1] For a bitch whose parents are registered, the fee is 50*p*. (this is called Class I registration), but for dogs whose parents are unregistered or unknown, the fee is £1 10*s* (Class II registration). The forms which must be completed are really self-explanatory, and the details required are obtainable both from the previous owner, and from the bitch's pedigree. It is wise to choose a rather unusual name when registering the bitch, and to give alternative suggestions in case the original selection has already been used, or is rejected for some reason.

If the bitch has already been registered by the previous owner, she should be transferred to the purchaser, and the fee for this is 7*s*. 6*d*. The form for transfer of a registered animal is obtainable from the Kennel Club, and the

[1] For latest list of Kennel Club fees *see* Addendum (page 96).

details can easily be filled in from the registration certificate. Sometimes breeders will lend a bitch for one or more litters, to be returned at the end of a mutually arranged period. This "loan of bitch", as it is called, has quite a number of advantages, but of course it is usually a temporary arrangement, although some "loans" end by being permanent. The loan of a bitch must be registered at the Kennel Club by the lender, who must state, among other details, the name and address of the borrower, the conditions, if any, of the loan, and the duration of the period.

It is a curious fact that the best show bitches are not necessarily the best broods, and many of the big winners in all breeds are produced by rather "ordinary" looking bitches, mated to the right dog, and beautifully bred themselves. The breeding (or blood-lines) of a bitch is all-important, and an experienced breeder in any breed can prophesy, with reasonable accuracy, what kind of puppies a bitch is likely to produce, from examining her pedigree. Whilst not necessarily a show specimen, she should not have any big faults of her breed. Where erect ears are required, it is a big mistake to buy a bitch with soft or floppy ears (this, of course, applies to an adult, or puppy over eight months, as ears are often uncertain in all breeds up till that age). She should conform, at least roughly, to the points of her breed, not be grossly over-size if small size is called for, and so on. It is a great mistake to think that anything is good enough to breed from. Very often bitches rather over-done in show points and exaggerated in type, make excellent broods. Beware, too, of the old-fashioned type of bitch; every breed has its fashions, and woe betide the beginner who invests in a bitch of this type—she will probably breed puppies like herself, and she will be no use to her new owner.

CHAPTER II

BREEDING: CHOICE OF SIRE

WE spoke of examining the pedigree. Let us look at it in rather greater detail. Although pedigree forms vary, in all of them the top half represents the sire's side and the bottom half, the dam's. If the bitch is reasonably well bred, you will find certain names recurring on both sides, and perhaps those of champions too. The presence of champions does not necessarily mean that the bitch will herself breed good puppies—much depends on the whole appearance of the pedigree, and not on individual dogs. The question of breeding is rather too big a subject with which to deal here, but, briefly, the more often a dog's name appears in a pedigree the more influence does that dog have on the resultant progeny.

A bitch which is in-bred (i.e. bred from closely related parents) is more likely to transmit her qualities, good or bad, to her offspring, especially if her mate is of similar breeding. In-breeding, especially close in-breeding, is rather a dangerous plan for the novice, as he knows so little of the dogs in the pedigree, and in-breeding emphasizes *everything*—faults as well as virtues. Some very minor fault in a dog in the pedigree can, if doubled and trebled, appear in a very exaggerated form in the puppies. Line-breeding (the pairing of two related animals but not so closely related as to entail in-breeding) is by far the wiser plan. While in-breeding involves such relationships as father-daughter, mother-son, brother-sister combinations, carried over several generations, line-breeding involves such matings as half-brother to half-sister, uncle to niece, granddaughter to grandfather, etc.

I believe there must be line-breeding (and in-breeding as well, by experienced breeders) to establish type and eventually a strain. Often the breeder of the bitch is the best person to advise as to a suitable stud dog. At all events, try to choose a dog whose pedigree has some of the best ancestors in your bitch's pedigree (in doggy parlance, is not an "outcross") and also has himself some, anyway, of the points in which your bitch fails. If she has, say, a poor coat, choose a dog which not only excels in coat himself, but is bred from dogs with this point. However, unless your bitch has a fair number of ancestors carrying good coats, only one or two of the puppies may inherit this factor, as so much depends on *both* blood lines and the bitch has an equal part to play. The whole subject of breeding is very complicated and, though some exhibitors seem to achieve their good results almost by accident, to be consistently successful, and build up a winning strain, needs much study, experience and experiment.

CHAPTER III

THE OESTRUM: SENDING TO THE STUD DOG

HAVING, after much thought and inquiry, decided on a dog which should suit the bitch, the next step is to arrange with the stud-dog owner. A popular sire should have his services booked well in advance, and the dog's owner should be told when the bitch is due in season. The age at which a bitch is ready to be bred from varies with the breed; in some of the bigger breeds, for instance, it is inadvisable to mate bitches before eighteen months or two years, whereas, with some toys, early mating is the rule, before the bones of the pelvis become too "set" for easy whelping. Broadly speaking, it is wiser to delay a first litter until the bitch is over a year old—until then the young bitch is undeveloped and it is a mistake to breed from an immature animal. If, therefore, the first oestrum (or season) occurs at six to eight months, the bitch can usually be mated safely at the next. The period between seasons varies very greatly, and some bitches only come in breeding-use once a year. With the smaller breeds, the first season usually occurs at six to eight months, but it is sometimes delayed until twelve or fifteen months or even later. Some very immature bitches may not come in season at all, and if a bitch shows no signs of doing so by fifteen months, it is advisable to consult a good veterinary surgeon on the subject. A bitch can usually be brought into season artificially, by treatment, and mated successfully at a later date.

The first signs of the oestrum vary—with some, there

is swelling and a clear discharge; with others, the first sign noted is a blood-coloured vaginal discharge, and the swelling takes place later. At all events, the wise owner will keep close watch on his bitch from six months onwards, as it is important to notice when the first signs appear. The stud-dog owner should be informed as soon as the red vaginal discharge is noticed (in doggy parlance, "showing colour") and, unless otherwise instructed, the bitch should be sent to the stud-dog's kennels on about the tenth day from the start of the coloured discharge, unless a very long journey is involved, when a day or two earlier is safer. Many owners prefer to accompany their bitches, and, if the bitch is shy, this is quite a good plan. In the case of a very nervous or highly strung bitch, tranquillisers may sometimes be necessary and the veterinary surgeon should be consulted. On the other hand, as the proper time for mating varies very greatly, not only from breed to breed, but also from bitch to bitch, it is very difficult to know whether the right day has been chosen. If one had been unlucky, several journeys may have to be made before the mating is accomplished successfully. Provided the kennel is a reputable one, it is far wiser to send the bitch in a secure box (often the owner of the stud dog will lend one if asked) and very handy travelling boxes can be made for small dogs from tea-chests.

In winter, there should be plenty of bedding; wheat straw is the best as it is more "springy" than blankets and absorbs the inevitable jolts of the journey better. In summer, several sacks form the best material, but, at any rate, something soft and comfortable should be provided. The provision of adequate ventilation is very important; during the winter it should not be so liberal as to chill the bitch (especially as the box may be left about in draughty stations), and during the summer it should be plentiful, as boxes are often stacked one on top of another. The box should be sufficiently big for the dog to stand erect and turn round with freedom. Travelling in very cold or very hot weather, unless essential, is to be deprecated, particularly in view of present travelling conditions. The box should be very plainly labelled, in large block capitals, preferably made with indian ink, and the words "Valuable Live Dog" displayed prominently. The name of the stud-dog owner-his telephone number if any, the station to which she is to be sent and any changes en route, must all be clearly set out. Be sure the box is securely fastened, as bitches in season often want to escape, and well-meaning porters sometimes open the box if everything is made too easy. Many valuable bitches have been lost from this cause. If a padlock is used, the key should be tied on securely, and not sent in advance to the stud-dog's owner, as it must be possible to open the box in an emergency (such as fire) en route. It is possible to insure dogs "higher value" rate and, where any change is involved, this is a wise precaution, as it does help to ensure more speedy transport.

The stud-dog owner should be advised beforehand as to the train on which the bitch is sent, and the probable time of her arrival. If a long journey is involved, it is often better to send bitches over-night, and this applies particularly during the crowded summer holiday months, as night travelling is cooler and quieter. Week-end journeys should be avoided if possible. Before sending, the bitch should be well exercised, be given a good meal and a drink. It is a help to the stud-dog owner if she wears a collar, as some bitches are very nervous of strangers. If she is a bad traveller, and is sick in train or car, chloretone capsules[1] (dose from three grains upwards, depending on size) an hour before the journey is an excellent plan. They are also useful for highly strung bitches which may be frightened by travelling.[2]

Perhaps I should add at this point that the bitch should be clean, well-groomed and free from external parasites before sending her to another kennel. All stud-dog owners have had experience of dirty bitches, probably infested with fleas and lice in addition, and as these pests are extremely contagious and prolific, neither the bitch nor her owner will be at all popular. It should not be necessary to add that every bitch sent away for mating should be in perfect health and with no signs of skin trouble. This is important, as outbreaks of distemper and "hard pad" in stud-dogs' kennels have been traced to visiting bitches. There are preparations on the market designed to discourage the attentions of male dogs but, needless to say, these must not be used on a bitch before mating.

In due course, if all is well, the stud-dog owner will tell you that the bitch has been mated. There are rare occasions when it is impossible to effect a mating—sometimes the bitch absolutely refuses service (this occasionally happens with sexually immature animals) or has a vaginal stricture (which should be dealt with by a veterinary surgeon) but, in the ordinary way, all should

[1] Chloretone is seldom available nowadays. There are numerous proprietary remedies for car sickness such as "Sea Legs", which are very good but great care should be taken with dosage and very small doses be given to begin with, sufficient for mild sedation but not enough to 'knock out' the dog (which sometimes happens with unwise administration!)

[2] I would not advise anyone nowadays to send a bitch by rail. The situation has radically changed since this book was first written. The bitch should be *taken* to the stud dog either by car or rail but not sent unaccompanied.

be successfully accomplished, and it is then the duty of the bitch's owner to send the stud fee, plus the return carriage. The bitch will usually be returned twenty-four hours or so after mating and, until all signs of the season have ceased, she must be kept closely confined, in case she is accidentally mated. Incidentally, if a *mésalliance* does occur, it is quite possible to prevent conception by an injection, which can be given by any veterinary surgeon. As this injection would also affect a legitimate mating, it can only be given when a litter is not desired and it should be given as soon as possible after the *mésalliance*.

If there is any reason to suspect worms, the bitch should be dosed for this as soon as the season is over, but it is unwise to delay this beyond the third week of pregnancy.

CHAPTER IV

FOR five or six weeks after mating there is no need to make any difference in the bitch's food and routine. On no account should exercise be neglected—up to the very last day or two she should have her walks, although, as she becomes heavy, it must necessarily be restricted, and she should not indulge in any galloping. For the last week or two, she may prefer to take sedate ambles round the garden, and in this matter her wishes should be respected. At the end of the fifth week or so, there will probably be some indications of her condition—she will be heavier, will probably drop appreciably in body, and her teats will be larger. If these signs are absent, it will not necessarily mean that she has failed to conceive, as some bitches show little or no signs of pregnancy, especially when there are only one or two puppies present in the uterus. It is not wise to feel bitches to see if they are in whelp, and the less the abdomen is touched and handled, the better. Should it be necessary to lift a heavily pregnant bitch—and it should be avoided whenever possible—it should be done carefully, gently and steadily. Pass the right hand between the bitch's front legs and grasp her outside leg firmly, and put the other hand round her hindquarters grasping her further hindleg, then, leaning her body towards you, lift her gently. This will obviate pressure on her abdomen. Going up and downstairs, jumping on a chair, if not too high, and so on, will not harm the average bitch, as the foeti are cushioned

23

in fluid against slight casual jolts of this kind, but she should not be allowed to squeeze under gates, through narrow openings, or be bumped by other dogs when playing.

Occasionally a bitch, especially a middle-aged one, will show signs of abortion about the fifth week (this is usually denoted by haemorrhage from the vagina). Expert treatment is often successful in such cases but a veterinary surgeon should be consulted immediately. Abortions later in pregnancy are usually due to specific diseases, such as distemper, or to accidents. All bitches in whelp should lead as placid a life as possible, and travelling should be avoided after the seventh week.

Some bitches lack appetite during the early weeks of pregnancy but, as the weeks pass, this usually remedies itself. "Morning sickness" is an early symptom of gestation, usually occurring about the third week. The normal bitch eats extremely well throughout the period, but slight inappetence need cause no concern, provided the bitch seems well in herself, and her temperature is normal. However, absolute refusal to eat (whether or not accompanied by fever) at about the sixth week is an ominous symptom and requires investigation by the veterinary surgeon. Many bitches have a clear mucoid discharge from the vagina, especially if the litter is a big one. No notice need be taken of this, but if it alters in character, becoming excessive, dark green, pinkish, or offensive, the bitch's temperature should be taken at once, and if over 39·5°C. (103°F.) the veterinary surgeon informed. The normal temperature is 38–38·5°C. (100·6–101·5°F.), but as a discharge of this nature usually means something is seriously wrong, fever, if present, will probably be 39·5–41°C. (103–105°F.), so anything under 39·5°C. (103°F.) is not of consequence. However, as such a discharge is very far from being normal, the temperature should be taken twice daily for the next few days, and the bitch kept under close observation as a precaution.

At five and a half weeks or so the diet requires attention, and four meals a day are not too many if the bitch is heavy in whelp. It is very important to remember that the unborn young must be fed via their mother, who can only give to them what she herself receives, and she, too, must be well-nourished if she is to fulfil her important functions properly.

The first meal of the day should consist of a liberal allowance of milk, either with or without porridge. Milk is a rich natural source of calcium, apart from its other qualities, and this mineral is essential for the puppies. During their intra-uterine life they draw very heavily on their dam for bone-formation, etc., and if she has to supply it unaided from her own resources, she may develop the dangerous condition of parturient eclampsia. It is impossible to over-emphasise the importance of plenty of milk both before and after whelping. The second meal in the day (for a dog about Terrier size) should consist of about half a pound of raw meat plus quarter of a pound of brown bread cubes. Moisten this with gravy and add a teaspoonful or more of cod liver oil plus specially prepared bone meal. Some bitches find cod liver oil too rich for easy digestion, and, in such cases, halibut liver oil should be substituted. It is essential to supply Vitamin D in either of these two forms as, apart from its own beneficial qualities, it is required for the absorption of the calcium content present in milk and bone meal.[1] For the third meal (this can be omitted if the litter looks like being a small one) give either egg and milk, or tripe and

[1] *See* Addendum, page 98 ("Vivomin")

bread, and, for the fourth meal, raw meat alone (half a pound for Terrier size).

The reason for giving four meals a day is in order to tax the bitch's digestive system as little as possible—if she is carrying a big litter, there is bound to be some pressure on the internal organs and it will be found that she is not able to take very much food at a time. Quality, rather than quantity, and concentrated nourishment should be the rule. Members of the Vit. B. Complex group (found in yeast among other substances) make a desirable supplement to the diet. As a bitch in whelp is always very thirsty plenty of water should always be available.

The period of gestation in the bitch is about nine weeks and a day, but many whelp a few days earlier or later. Premature puppies need quiet, warmth and the minimum of interference, but provided they are not more than five days too early in arriving there is no reason why they should not survive, and I have had at least two litters which lived, though born six days too soon. Veterinary surgeons differ in their opinion of the gravity —or otherwise—of delayed whelping, and while some think five days is the limit of safety, others think that interference is only required if the bitch is more than a week over-due. With first whelpings it is certainly wiser to report if a bitch is more than four days over-due and, with experienced broods, five days. Of course, if there is any previous history of the bitch having produced dead puppies after a delayed parturition, a veterinary surgeon should be consulted in the later weeks of gestation, with a view to terminating pregnancy if he considers it advisable. Sometimes delay is caused by the death of foeti at the time they should be born, and such cases need qualified treatment.

CHAPTER V

THE VETERINARY SURGEON AND THE BREEDER

I HAVE already mentioned the necessity of calling in qualified veterinary advice, and as this recommendation will often be repeated, I think it desirable to go into this matter in rather more detail. Many breeders, even nowadays, appear to dislike and distrust the veterinary profession, and will often boast that they "never have a vet on the place". Such people may have had very unfortunate experiences with veterinary surgeons and consider they know better, or be careless and casual people. Veterinary surgeons themselves differ, and, considering all have to pass through the same training, it is rather remarkable that such great variations exist, although it is of course the same with the sister profession, human medicine. I am not slighting a profession to which I owe so much when I say that many veterinary surgeons are not interested in small-animal practice, sometimes saying so quite openly, and, as a result, are not very successful with this branch of their profession. I rather think that a first-class practitioner, really interested and skilled with small animals, is born, not made. One's opinion of the veterinary profession is, willy-nilly, formed very much by one's own personal practitioner, and, if one has a brilliant veterinarian, one tends, perhaps, to think all are alike or vice versa.

The choice of a first-class veterinary surgeon may be difficult in certain parts of the country, and the nearest is not always the best but, as this choice may mean the saving of valuable canine lives—or the reverse—it is well worth making an effort to find one in whom one may safely put one's confidence. It is often a good plan to ask several well-known breeders: their views may vary and it is sometimes necessary to take them with a grain of salt! but if the consensus of opinion points to one surgeon being extremely good—or the reverse—it is a fairly reliable guide. Having (possibly by trial and error) found the best veterinary surgeon in the area, you must do your part by trusting him, giving him your confidence and your co-operation, and by implicit reliance on his judgment and skill. Nothing annoys a good veterinary surgeon more than to have his client attempt to diagnose (usually quite wrongly) the animal's ailment, or to "instruct" him in the line of treatment to be followed. This is a far more common procedure than one would think. I have been told many times by veterinary surgeons that dog breeders and owners, as a class, are not very popular clients, as they often consider they know far more than the surgeon, and he is sometimes called in merely to "confirm" the breeder's diagnosis! The habit, followed by some, of consulting a different practitioner each time, or going to one for a serious illness, and to another for a minor one, is hardly likely to endear the client. Besides being contrary to professional etiquette, mutual confidence and respect are unlikely to be established. Another very important point: if a veterinary surgeon is called in at all, his instructions or advice must be scrupulously followed (and not "interpreted" according to the breeder's own ideas) and no drugs should be given, except those prescribed or given by the practitioner.

I mention this as, all too often, both breeders and private owners secretly give their dogs proprietary medicines in such illnesses as distemper. This is not only unfair to the practitioner in charge of the case, but can be very dangerous. If a veterinary surgeon merits one's whole confidence (and that is why the choice of a first-class one must be made with such care) he *must* have entire charge of his patients and the nursing, treatment, etc., must be approved by him and carried out under his supervision. A keen *modern* practitioner can be of the very greatest help, not only to the "one-dog" man, but also to the kennel owner, as his work lies not only in treating disease, but in preventing it, and in educating the dog-owning public in the maintenance of health. He should be permitted scope for this, and not be regarded, merely, as someone to be consulted in actual illness. Nowadays, with so many dangerous diseases about, the more a kennel (however small) is kept under veterinary supervision, the better. And do not refer to a veterinary surgeon as a "vet". This abbreviation is extremely unpopular with the profession, and deservedly so, I think. It is a survival of the old days and is better forgotten.

CHAPTER VI

PREPARATIONS FOR WHELPING

ABOUT a week before the bitch is due, some preparations should be made. If the bitch is to whelp in a kennel, she should be given one to herself a week or two before the puppies are due. Both the kennel itself and the whelping-bed should be scrupulously clean and should be freshly scrubbed for the occasion. It is a good plan to keep the whelping-bed for the actual event and give the bitch another roomy bed in the meantime in order to keep the former perfectly clean. The whelping-bed should

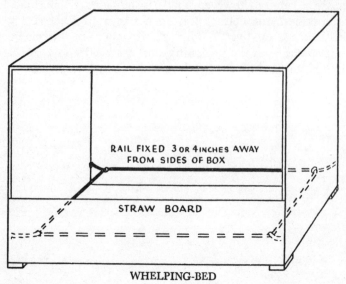

RAIL FIXED 3 OR 4 INCHES AWAY
FROM SIDES OF BOX

STRAW BOARD

WHELPING-BED

be of very ample proportions—a large packing case on its side is excellent and provides a roof and sides for cold weather. A board, about six inches wide, should be fitted across the front of the box, at the bottom, to prevent bedding (and puppies) from falling out. Some breeders fix a rail round the inside of the box, two or three inches from the sides and a few inches from the floor to prevent puppies being crushed against the sides by an inexpert dam. The bed should be prepared by lining it very thickly with brown paper and newspaper, making several layers. Extra newspapers should be at hand to replace soiled ones while whelping is in progress. If the bitch is to whelp in the house (and, with a first litter, this is very advisable as the bitch can be kept under observation more easily) I use a very large oval basket, also thickly lined with newspapers. I find this makes by far the best surface for parturition: it is hygienic, provides a semi-firm surface, is not too cold, can be easily renewed and does not stick to the puppies' wet bodies. I also provide a small clean sack or blanket for the bitch to use until actual labour begins, as newspaper is very uncosy.

A day or two before the bitch is due to whelp, the abdominal hair in long-coated breeds should be removed, as dirt and worm ova are all too easily picked up, especially with dogs low to the ground. In addition, the abdomen and parts round and under the tail should be washed in a solution of pure soap flakes and weak Dettol and thoroughly dried. Although bathing a pregnant bitch is not desirable, she should be bodily clean and free from external parasites. If parturition is delayed, the local cleansing of abdomen, etc., may have to be repeated more than once. It should, of course, be done with great gentleness.

It is a wise precaution to take the bitch's temperature for a week before whelping. It is usual for the temperature to fall to 37°C. (99°F.) or less: when whelping is imminent, there is normally a still further drop to 36·5°C. (98°F.) or 36°C. (97°F.) If, on the other hand, there is a rise in temperature, it is an ominous symptom, and all-too often means trouble of some kind.

Although it is often recommended that bitches should be given castor oil before whelping, this is not a plan which I follow. It is, however, important that the bitch should not be constipated before parturition and, to this end, the diet should be rather sloppy during the last few days (for example, the meat can be minced) and olive oil given as a laxative if necessary.

CHAPTER VII

WHELPING

THE onset of parturition is shown by great restlessness on the part of the bitch, relaxation and swelling of the external genitalia, a desire for seclusion and often (but not invariably) refusal of food. She should be shut in a kennel or whelping-room (having first been allowed to relieve herself) as otherwise the parturient bitch has a way of crawling under kennels to make her own whelping arrangements! An unobtrusive eye must be kept on proceedings—this is specially important if it is a first litter. If the bitch is whelping in the house (and it is, of course, far easier to observe in such circumstances) one can write letters or read a book without appearing to be watching, as some bitches resent this. Unless the weather is very warm, artificial heat must be provided in the whelping-room or -kennel, as warmth is, in my view, essential for new-born whelps. A hot bottle (well-covered) should be provided and this can be slipped into the whelping-box when the first puppy has arrived.

The signs of imminent labour are: shivering, great restlessness, panting, scratching or tearing up of paper and obvious discomfort. Actual labour begins with the bitch straining (these rhythmic uterine contractions look rather as though the bitch is constipated) and it is important to notice the time at this juncture. The straining becomes more frequent, and increases in intensity, until (with normal labour) the water bag appears. This prepares the way for the puppy, but the former is rarely

33

seen intact as the bitch ruptures it with her teeth. However, a sudden rush of fluid, which the bitch will lick up, means that the long-awaited moment is approaching. On the other hand, if the bitch goes on straining, looks anxious, and no puppy appears after about one hour, some investigation must be made to see whether a foetus is present in the vagina.

Some bitches take longer to produce their young than others, and this is often so with a first litter, but after an hour and a half of forcible and continuous straining, the puppy should certainly have passed through the pelvic opening and be in the vagina, even if unborn. Examination of bitches by amateurs should never be undertaken if it is avoidable, and if the veterinary surgeon is readily available, and near at hand, he should be called. But many whelpings take place at night, the veterinary surgeon may be some considerable distance away, and he will then appreciate a preliminary investigation. The hands should be thoroughly scrubbed with plenty of soap and water, and, without drying them, the index finger should be inserted *gently* into the vagina. Extreme care is essential. You may feel, within reach of your finger, a smooth wet "object". Do not push or press, but withdraw your finger and wait a few minutes. Then feel again, and, if there has been appreciable movement, the foetus feeling much nearer than it did, in all probability the puppy will soon be born. On the other hand, if the foetus is exactly in the same position, and the bitch has been straining strongly in the meantime, the veterinary surgeon must be called. Similarly, if no puppy can be felt, it is urgent to obtain qualified assistance immediately. Never attempt to do anything yourself on these occasions. Manipulation of any kind, with finger or (worse still) forceps, is extremely dangerous and must be left to the veterinary surgeon.

It will be seen why I emphasised the necessity of noticing the time when the bitch starts straining. Old-fashioned dog books, written when the veterinary profession was more concerned with horses than dogs, often recommend all sorts of investigations and explorations into the vagina; in fact, one well-known book seems to consider that veterinary attention is only required for Cæsarian sections! In those days the breeder had, all too often, to rely on his own scanty veterinary knowledge, with the consequent death of many valuable bitches and puppies. Nowadays, with a highly skilled profession at our disposal, the less we interfere with our bitches, the better.

Should the veterinary surgeon have to be called (and, except in some breeds, such as French Bulldogs, this a rare occurrence) some preparations should be made for his visit. He will need a firm table, covered with a thick dust-sheet and newspaper on top, a good light (especially if it is a night whelping), Dettol (the antiseptic most favoured for obstetric cases), one or two dishes to act as receivers, cotton wool and, of course, excellent washing facilities and plenty of hot water. If everything is ready beforehand, it will help the busy practitioner. Incidentally, it is always wiser to consult with your veterinary surgeon beforehand if any trouble is anticipated with a whelping. Scottish Terriers, Dachshunds, Bulldogs, Pekingese and Boxers may have a difficult labour. However, many breeds whelp with the greatest ease, and it is usually a normal and natural process.

There is another condition often met with in some breeds which also requires veterinary attention. I refer to uterine inertia, perhaps one of the most trying of labour difficulties. With this, the straining is either very slight, or absent, and the uterine contractions must therefore be induced if possible, and other measures employed, possibly involving Cæsarian section. The latter operation, while still a very serious one, if performed by a first-class surgeon is fairly safe nowadays, but it is, of course, a major one, and the bitch should be in good condition, and not exhausted by fruitless straining, hour after hour. Forceps deliveries, which sound awe-inspiring to the novice, can also be very successful in *skilled* hands and provided the veterinarian is called in time. To sum up: if, after about an hour of forcible and continuous straining no puppy has appeared, investigate, and, if necessary, call your veterinary surgeon *immediately*. Do the same if straining is feeble or absent. And consult him in advance if you have a breed in which trouble may be anticipated.

Presuming all is well, within about twenty minutes (sometimes less) to about an hour, the first puppy will arrive. It is easy to see when it is about to be born, as the bitch will become more agitated, will be busy licking herself up, or examining her hindquarters, and obviously preparing for the birth. The observer may be unaware that the whelp has actually arrived, as the bitch may be so busy rupturing the foetal membrane (in which every puppy is born) and licking and cleaning it up, that the first knowledge he has is a rather gurgling cry from the puppy as it takes its first breath. The foetal membrane encloses the puppy like a bag, and it is essential for it to be removed as soon as the puppy is born to enable it to breathe. Sometimes the dam makes no attempt to do this, and the puppy—a black, shiny object—lies unattended. It is here that prompt attention will save the whelp's life. The breeder must himself break open the membrane over the puppy's head and, if necessary, open its mouth gently with the tip of his finger. Often this is all that is required, and the dam will attend to the rest, but sometimes it is necessary to carry on. The membrane should be gently stripped from the puppy's body and the infant dried on a rough towel.

If it seems reluctant to breathe, open its mouth and breathe into it, tap its chest, and toss it from hand to hand, the hands being held about six inches apart. If these efforts are successful, it will soon cry, and this is essential in order to clear the tiny lungs of mucous. The puppy will be attached, by the umbilical cord, to the placenta (or afterbirth) which is still within the mother's body. The cord is usually bitten through by the bitch, after she has removed the membrane and, even if an inexperienced dam does not deal with this immediately, it is advisable to wait to see if she will do so once the placenta (afterbirth) is expelled. If it is necessary to cut the cord (and this is always required with the short-nosed breeds such as Pekingese) tie a piece of white cotton very tightly about an inch and a half away from the puppy, and cut it on the dam's side. In the rare event of haemorrhage, tincture of iodine should be applied. Some breeders always remove the placenta but I never do so myself, as I believe in the minimum of interference. Until the next puppy is born the dam will be busy with her baby, licking it, tossing it about (this stimulates the circulation) and drying it. The puppy should cry within a few minutes of birth, and if it does not do so, the mouth should be opened with the tip of one's little finger, which is usually all that is required.

If the whelps are numerous, the bed will become wet as time goes on, so, if it is possible to do this without disturbing the dam, clean newspaper should be put in, over the soiled, if it is not easy to remove the latter. It is still necessary to watch the clock each time labour begins for a new arrival, as sometimes a bitch whelps several puppies with great ease and has difficulty over a later one. Occasionally a bitch has trouble in the final expulsion of a puppy, and the foetus will be seen "half in and half out". In such an event, after waiting a moment to see whether she can expel it herself, the visible part of the puppy should be gently but firmly grasped, and slowly and steadily drawn out *as and when* the bitch strains, and never between times.

Puppies very long "on the way" or born minus membrane (as sometimes happens) are in great danger of being suffocated or drowned. Sometimes bitches have too much uterine fluid, which results in dropsical or drowned puppies being born. This difficulty can usually be dealt with by a first-class veterinary surgeon if he is consulted beforehand.

Whelping usually lasts several hours, and, with a prolonged parturition, even if all is going well, the bitch may become exhausted, and she should be given drinks of glucose and milk from time to time. This is light, and easily digested, and is preferable to egg and milk. The milk should be cold, as warm milk is apt to dull the labour pains. The puppies should be encouraged to feed from the mother soon after birth, as this action has a beneficial stimulant effect on the uterus, aiding contractions, and thus leading to an earlier successful conclusion to the whelping.

When the last whelp is presumed to have arrived the dam should be let out to relieve herself; she will be very reluctant to leave her family, and will probably have to be carried or led out. She should wear a coat if the weather is cold or wet, as natural resistance is temporarily much lowered by the strain of whelping. During her absence the puppies should be gently removed and placed in a basket on a warmed blanket, and the soiled newspaper taken out of the whelping-bed. It should be replaced by a flat, firm mattress, made either from a blanket or sack (both spotlessly clean, of course), thinly filled with woodwool, and made to fit neatly in the bed. The surface should not be too soft and billowy or the puppies will get lost in the folds, and it should form a flat, firm surface. The mattress should be warm. Transfer the puppies carefully to the clean bed, handling each as gently and lightly as possible, with just a brief glance to see the sex, whether there are abnormalities or deformities, and whether dew-claws (those little extra nails which grew inside the leg) are present on the hindlegs. Everything should be ready, so that the transfer can be made as quickly as possible, but remember, when handling the puppies, to move them slowly; sudden movements and snatching up a puppy are not desirable. They should not be handled in front of the dam unless essential, as this gives the most sweet-natured bitch actual pain, and some dams are apt to turn "cannibalistic" if their puppies are interfered with.

CHAPTER VIII

THE FIRST WEEK AFTER WHELPING

FOR the first three days after whelping the bitch should not be given solid food, as she is often slightly feverish. Her diet should consist of frequent drinks of warm milk (I give about five bowls a day) to which one or more eggs may be added. Where possible, prepared milk food is preferable to cow's milk. Some people add bicarbonate of soda in an effort to prevent acidity in the bitch's milk, not realising that it is normal for the latter to be acid. Much damage can be caused by giving alkalines in a misdirected effort to correct a perfectly natural condition, which cannot possibly harm the puppies. When people lose whelps from what they think is acidity, the cause is far more likely to be from streptococcal or staphylococcal infection. The symptoms of this are puppies dying or "fading out", usually within the first week or so, of birth. The whelps seem perfectly well when they arrive, but, after two or three days, they lose interest in sucking, are obviously not thriving, and all-too-often begin crying in a pointless and continuous fashion. This condition is invariably fatal, if untreated, and it is impossible to remedy the trouble without penicillin. If any puppy shows these ominous signs, the veterinary surgeon should be consulted; an experienced owner can give the injections himself, but otherwise the appropriate course will be given by the surgeon. Bitches which produce puppies affected in this way can themselves be treated before being mated, and if one has reason to suspect this very common trouble, or hepatitis (*see* Chapter XVI) a veterinary surgeon should be consulted.

In the ordinary way, however, the puppies will thrive, with a proud and happy mother, and, during their early infancy, require little attention. The dam will probably have black diarrhoea for a day or two after whelping; this should not be interfered with unless it continues for more than forty-eight hours, when a small dose of castor oil should be given. Her temperature should be taken twice daily for at least a week after parturition. There is often slight fever (up to 39°C. [102·4°F.]) but if it rises to 39·5°C. (103°F.), especially if accompanied by shivering and refusal of food, the veterinary surgeon should at once be informed, as a placenta may be retained, or a dead foetus be present in the uterus. Neglect to obtain prompt professional aid may lead to the death of the bitch from septicaemia, and delay is dangerous.

Provided the temperature is normal, the bitch can return to solid food by the fourth day, by way of fish and/or rabbit. The nursing bitch must be really well-fed, and five meals a day are not too many if she is to do justice to a big litter. For the first meal, give a generous allowance of warm milk, with, or without porridge; for the second, raw meat, brown bread, cod liver oil and bone meal; for the third, tripe or fish; for the fourth, raw meat alone; and, last thing at night, warm milk, with one or more eggs added. There is an erroneous idea that bitches do not feed their offspring at night, but actually they feed them regularly throughout the twenty-four hours in early infancy, and the milk given at about 11 p.m. will help the bitch during her nightly ministrations. Milk and raw meat are the best foods for ensuring a liberal supply of bitch's milk.

With a big litter, the question of a foster-mother must be considered. Personally, although I have reared many big litters, I have never used one, although I believe they are very successful, as I prefer to supplement by hand-feeding, if the litter is large. Although this is a tedious task, it is interesting and well worthwhile, and effectually relieves the strain on the dam. As the same methods apply if the dam dies, it may be useful to describe them briefly. I use full-cream baby milk food (the brand I use for hand-feeding is rather expensive but is a particularly rich kind, meant for delicate human babies). This, during feeding, should be kept at blood-heat, so it is best to stand the vessel in a basin of hot water to keep it at the correct temperature. The milk should be mixed to the same consistency as the evaporated variety and then thinned very slightly so that it resembles very rich creamy cow's milk.[1] Add medicinal glucose (allow a saltspoonful per puppy for small breeds) and give a teaspoonful or more (depending on breed) of this mixture to each puppy, using an old-fashioned medicine dropper with a rubber bulb. It is best to feed each puppy on the hot water-bottle and not pick them up if you can help it. Open the pup's mouth, put the dropper in, and feed *slowly*, allowing the puppy time to swallow and breathe. He may protest at first, but he will quickly get used to it. Be careful not to give too much. If this is supplementary feeding, choose the puppies in the litter which look the thinnest and smallest, and try to keep to the same ones each time. It will be necessary to feed them every two hours during the day and every three hours at night. It is a good idea to make a supply of milk food for the night, put it in a previously warmed thermos

[1] *See* Appendix.

flask, fill a second flask with boiling water, and sleep with an alarm clock! It does not take long to feed from the previously prepared flask, use water from the other to clean the puppy up (if it is being entirely hand-reared) and to wash out the medicine dropper. After ten days the night feeds are cut down to one at midnight, one at 4 a.m. and one at 8 a.m. After a fortnight there is no need to feed at night at all. Crookes' halibut liver oil emulsion should be added to all milk feeds, both for hand-reared puppies and for supplementary feeding. This emulsion is specially prepared for babies, and is readily miscible with water or milk, which does not apply to other preparations. From two drops (depending on breed) should be given per puppy, twice a day, and it can be given from a day old.

Whether the hand-feeding is supplementary or entire, the same rules apply, but, if the dam is dead, or unable to rear or look after the puppies at all, they must be kept very warm, and, after feeding, the abdomen should be gently rubbed in a circular direction until the bowels act. The natural orifices must be cleaned with cotton wool dipped in a mild antiseptic (the puppies must not be made too wet) and carefully dried with dry wool. It is a good plan to dust the whelps' "tummies" with boracic powder before replacing in the nest. At three weeks, scraped raw meat can be given, as with normally reared puppies. Hand-fed whelps, properly cared for and kept warm, should do well, and I have found them more forward in intelligence than the normally-reared puppy. Remember that everything used for them must be kept scrupulously clean. The medicine dropper should be thoroughly washed in soap and water after use, and kept immersed in cold boiled water in a covered cup, and the milk food be made at least once a day (in hot weather it should be freshly made for every meal) and kept covered in a cool place. Before fresh milk food is made, the basin should be well washed and then scalded. If scrupulous cleanliness is observed, hand-fed puppies are unlikely to suffer from diarrhoea or "tummy upsets", but it is important to remember to give the meals regularly, to give at the right temperature and not to give either too much or too little.

To return to our normally reared puppies. When they are three to five days old, their dew-claws should be removed and, in a breed where this is required, their tails docked. Although many breeders carry out this small operation themselves, it is not advisable for an amateur to attempt it. It is possible for a puppy to die of hae-morrhage or shock, and, all-too-often, the dew-claws are not properly removed, and grow again. So I suggest that a veterinary surgeon is called in for this small operation; it is an inexpensive one and better left in skilled hands. Although many people have only the dew-claws on the hind legs removed, I prefer to have those on the front legs amputated in addition, but of course this depends on the breed. It gives a cleaner line to the leg and, if left on, they sometimes get torn in later life. The dam should be removed well out of sight and sound of her offspring. After the little operation the puppies should have a clean towel placed under them in the whelping-bed, and the mother should not be allowed to return to them until active bleeding has ceased. There is seldom any hae-morrhage worth mentioning, but if there is, tincture of iodine should be applied. As the removal of the dew-claws is a slight shock to the system, the puppies should be kept extra warm afterwards.

It is advisable to feel the bitch's milk-glands from time to time during the first week to make sure they are all soft and pliable, as sometimes, especially if the puppies are small and weakly, one or more teats become hard and congested, and if this is neglected there is a danger of mastitis. In such an event, the milk gland should be massaged with olive oil or vaseline, and the milk drawn off with the fingers. If steps are taken at once, the glands should be normal in twenty-four hours, and the whelps should be encouraged to suck from the affected teats. Puppies' nails grow at astonishing speed after the first week, so, at about ten days, and thereafter once a week, they should be trimmed; it is easy to avoid the quick, which is quite obvious at this age, and looks pink and only the white curving tip should be snipped off. Neglect to do this will lead to the milk-glands becoming lacerated by the sharp talons, and the bitch may refuse to feed her young altogether.

Some highly strung bitches become very excited after whelping, and are most upset if the puppies cry, sometimes even refusing to let them suck, and are apparently unable to settle down. Such dams should be given a small dose of Parke Davis' chloretone[1] in capsule form—the dose is from three grains for small dogs.

More recently, preparations of the "tranquilliser" type have been found very useful in this type of case. You should consult your veterinary surgeon about this as these drugs are obtainable only on prescription.

---

[1] Chloretone has to a large extent been replaced by other and newer agents, such as acetylpromazine. Both preparations need a veterinary surgeon's prescription.

CHAPTER IX

SOMETIMES young puppies will be found to have a most unpleasant "scabby" rash within a few days of birth. With long-haired breeds this can be felt as thickened patches and pustules. This is due to maternal inexperience, and is caused by the dam not having licked her puppies properly clean after birth. It is of little consequence, and the scabs dry up and drop off in a short time, but their disappearance can be hastened by the application of vaseline.

Weighing the puppies at birth, and thereafter once weekly, is a good plan, as it enables the breeder to note the progress of each individual puppy. A record of these weights should be kept, and it is also useful to include any other relevant particulars, especially as the puppies get older—colour, marking, sex, whether the parturition was easy or difficult, individual idiosyncrasies, progress, any ailments, etc. This is a great help on future occasions. I keep a special book in which to record these details and I find I am always looking over past entries. Anything abnormal about the bitch should also be noted—if, for instance, she was at all feverish after whelping, if she had plenty of milk, etc., etc.

New-born puppies are unable to hear or see until they are about ten days old, and live entirely by instinct —that of self-preservation. After ten days, however, they begin to assume an individuality. *Sudden* noises and vibrations should be avoided from the start, but, after a fortnight, the babies should be gradually accustomed to the sounds and sights of everyday life. If a door bangs near a puppy it will often be seen to start violently, and this slight shock to the system is not desirable. Puppies should be frequently talked to and gently handled, when they are being attended, and this will help to prevent possible future shyness.

Novices sometimes become alarmed at the twitching and jerking seen in young puppies when asleep, but this, of course, is a natural phenomenon.

An unobtrusive eye should be kept on the puppies during the first fortnight, to see all are sucking properly and are warm. A puppy which is constantly crying and cold is not thriving and, if necessary, it will have to be removed from the dam and wrapped up in cotton wool on a hot water-bottle. An effort should be made to hand-feed it, if it has obviously not been having enough nourishment from the dam, and it should be fed in the same way as suggested for hand-reared puppies, with the difference that a few drops of brandy can be added to the first feed or two if the puppy seems moribund. Occasionally bitches have insufficient milk for their offspring, and, if plenty of raw meat and milk make no difference to the supply, the puppies will certainly be in the state described above and must be either wholly or partially hand-fed; in such cases, the puppies can usually stay with the dam, who keeps them warm and clean.

It is extremely important that, throughout lactation, the dam should have cod liver oil and bone meal daily.[1] There is a very dangerous condition known as parturient eclampsia due to lack of calcium in the bitch's blood-

[1] "Vivomin", as previously explained, should be used instead of cod liver oil and bone meal.

stream. As the calcium is excreted, via the milk, to the puppies, she must be given sufficient to replace her own supply. Milk, bone meal, and Vitamin D (in the form of halibut liver oil or cod liver oil), is essential for nursing mothers. Eclampsia is more common in highly-strung and nervy mothers, and they are usually the most devoted dams, with very fat puppies—nourished, not wisely but too well, at the bitch's expense. It is rather unusual in a first lactation and is more likely to happen when the puppies are two or three weeks old. The symptoms vary, but they include convulsions (eclamptic fits, which resemble epileptic fits and must not be confused with hysteria) in which the bitch lies on her side and foams at the mouth. If these take place at night, in her kennel, you may be unaware of them. The temperature is usually subnormal, the bitch looks dazed and exhausted, she walks stiffly and seems disinclined to move, she may vomit and looks very depressed. If the condition occurs, the veterinary surgeon should at once be informed. The specific treatment is calcium injected subcutaneously, and speed is essential, as eclampsia can prove rapidly fatal if neglected.

CHAPTER X

THE dam will keep the puppies' bed clean until about three weeks of age, but their mattress will require changing once a week or so. If the bitch has whelped indoors, and it is desirable to move mother and puppies into a kennel, the move should be delayed, if possible, until the whelps are a week old, unless the weather is warm. A stove should be placed in the kennel beforehand to heat it (except in the summer) and a bed should be prepared which will be cosy and draught-proof. With small or medium breeds, a tea-chest or packing-case, placed on its side, with a board six to eight inches wide nailed across the bottom to keep the puppies safely in, will be found to be excellent. In winter, a sack or blanket should be hung across the front, allowing the bitch just enough room to get in and out, and this will keep them cosy. In extra cold weather, blankets or sacks should be hung all round the box, covering the surface entirely, to "insulate" it. If a hot water-bottle is given in addition, there will be no need to use a stove while the kennel is occupied, which, owing to the risk of fire, is a dangerous procedure. The box should have a thick layer of sawdust at the bottom, then newspaper, and finally the mattress. After three weeks, wheat straw or (better still) woodwool can be used, and this will need changing at least every three days, and probably more often, until the puppies are old enough to get out of their bed. When the latter is changed, the bottom of the floor should be wiped over with a cloth wrung out in diluted lysol and the sawdust renewed. It is a good idea to treat the floors of sleeping boxes and kennels first with linseed oil and then two coats of varnish, as it forms a non-absorbent surface.

When the puppies' eyes open (at from about ten days old to sixteen days) they will soon be exploring their new world and, to begin with, their dam will be very upset when they tumble out on to the floor, especially as they will find it difficult to get back. A "step" made of a box or similar object, should be placed outside the straw board; the babies very quickly learn to climb on to it, and get back to bed without help.

Sometimes puppies' eyes seem glued up and show no signs of opening by the fourteenth day. Bathing with warm boracic lotion and (if necessary) anointing the lids with "golden eye ointment" is usually all that is required.

CHAPTER XI

WEANING

PERHAPS the most important early step in a puppy's life is the change-over from mother's milk to solid or semi-solid food, and most of the upsets which so often accompany the important process of weaning are caused by too much haste and too much food. It is essentially a *gradual* process, and diarrhoea, etc., should be unknown.

The age at which weaning begins depends on the size of the litter. If it is big, it should not be delayed beyond three weeks, but, with a small litter, four weeks will be time enough. I use baby milk food, mixed to the consistency of extra creamy milk for the first fortnight, after this, to the consistency of creamy cow's milk.[1] I begin with three daily feeds—morning, noon and night—feeding each puppy separately and adding one drop of halibut liver oil emulsion (Crookes)[2] per puppy, to the morning and night feeds. I find it a good idea to take each puppy on my lap, and present it with a spoonful of warm milk food. Usually the smell is sufficient, after I have, if necessary, "directed" the puppy's head down to the spoon. If the puppy is slow, a little milk can be smeared on its nose. When the bitch is a good mother, and has plenty of milk, you may find the youngsters do not seem to want the extra feeding, and are most reluctant to take it; sooner or later, they will need it, and, in the meantime, it can be offered, preferably when the dam has been absent from them for a time. Most bitches feed their puppies at very regular intervals and it is fairly easy to

[1] *See* Appendix.

[2] Halibut liver oil is not necessary as baby milk foods all have added vitamins.

"time" your feeds so that they do not coincide with their maternal nourishment. The quantities of milk given to each puppy will naturally depend on the breed; for medium sized breeds, five or six teaspoonfuls per puppy, per feed, will be found to be about right, but in the case of a puppy much bigger than its fellows, more should be given. All quantities must be varied according to individual size and progress. I feel it is very important to feed each puppy separately, not only from the beginning, but throughout, otherwise it is impossible to avoid one greedy puppy getting more than its share and a small delicate one not getting enough.

The milk food should be freshly made for each meal in the summer. In the winter, except in a warm spell, a supply can be made for the day, and kept covered, but it should not be kept over-night. It should be well stirred before each feed, and the best way to warm it is to stand the basin in a bowl of boiling water.

A week later the puppies can have their first taste of meat. I use "human-consumption" horse-meat only, and feel it is very dangerous to give young puppies slaughterer's meat, especially uncooked. The horse-meat should be used raw, and scraped till soft and to the consistency of butter, with a tablespoon used like a knife. A tiny scrap (about the size of one's finger-nail) should be given to each puppy twice a day, alternating with the milk food. Each puppy gets, therefore, five "meals" a day—milk, meat, milk, milk and meat again. As a rule they show no hesitation about taking meat, but, if necessary, it can be rubbed on their gums, or a tiny fragment popped into their mouths. The meat should be very gradually increased until, after a week (in medium-sized breeds like Terriers), the amount is a teaspoonful per puppy, twice a day. It is very important to make the increase very gradual, as much harm can be caused by a sudden and sharp increase. It is now possible to use butcher's meat, although this is rather expensive, but whatever is used, it is most important to avoid knacker's meat. Some puppies will not take raw meat at first, but a little perseverance and patience is usually all that is required. Raw meat is a dog's natural diet and infinitely preferable to cooked, but when the latter is necessary the meat should be very lightly cooked in boiling water to "seal in" all the juices. It will be appreciated that these feeds are supplementary—to begin with—to those given by the dam, but, as the supplementary food is gradually increased, the demand made by the youngsters on the dam decreases little by little, and her milk-glands slowly dry up. Weaning should be a slow process, and the dam's instincts are the best guide; she can be trusted to feed her puppies as and when she will; it will be found she does not feed them so often and, sooner or later, will lie away from them at night, even if she has no alternative bed (and, from three weeks onwards, she should have another bed, preferably out of reach of her puppies, to which she can go). If she starts to growl at them the time has come for her to be removed entirely at night, and also during the day, except when she wants to feed them.

Some bitches vomit partially digested food for their babies; this is a natural and not a disgusting habit! However, it is not one of which I much approve, as, even if partially digested, what the bitch has been eating would not always be suitable for the puppies.

At five weeks of age a small teaspoonful of crumbled brown bread can be added to one of the milk feeds (amounts are for Terrier size) and egg (in the proportion of half egg, half milk) to another. Allow one egg between two puppies at this age. Fish can be substituted, if eggs are short. At this time, too, bone-forming supplements must be added, in the shape of prepared bone meal (the same as that used for the dam during pregnancy and lactation)—a pinch on the meat feed for each puppy, increasing gradually until, at eight weeks, each puppy receives one teaspoonful.[1] Quantities of all foods should be increased by about a teaspoonful extra per week (more for bigger pups—size is often unequal in a litter) and two drops of Crookes' halibut liver oil emulsion added twice a day for each puppy from five to eight weeks. (At eight weeks, cod liver oil or halibut liver oil can replace the emulsion.) At six weeks, the amount of meat will be about a dessert-spoonful twice a day for Terrier size (it can be finely minced from six weeks onwards). At seven weeks, two teaspoonfuls of porridge (or crumbled brown bread) can be added for each puppy, to the first milk feed.

The daily "menu" will then be roughly on the following lines: For the first meal, porridge and milk; for the second, one and a half dessertspoonfuls finely minced raw meat, with half a teaspoonful each of cod liver oil and bone meal (this can be increased to a teaspoonful each at eight weeks) or three drops of halibut liver oil. For the third meal, egg and milk (or fish); for the fourth, two teaspoon-fuls crumbled brown bread and milk; and, for the final meal, a dessertspoonful and a half of finely minced meat.

At about eight or nine weeks, add corn-flakes (broken up to begin with) to the egg and milk feed. All quantities should be gradually increased each week and it is impossible to give specific amounts as so much depends on the individual puppy and its progress. It is very important that it should be plump and well-covered, but not flabbily fat, as too much weight in the stomach causes

[1] Where halibut liver oil (or cod liver oil) and bone meal are referred to "Vivomin", "Vionate" or "Stress" should be used.

the front legs to bend, which may result in crooked fronts. At about ten weeks I drop one of the meals, and give four as follows: Breakfast, porridge and milk[1]; dinner, brown bread (either crumbled or cut up very small) and mince, moistened with gravy, plus bone meal and cod liver oil; tea, shredded wheat (broken up) with milk, or corn-flakes and milk; supper, mince, moistened with gravy, with or without brown bread, depending on individual condition.

It is important to remember that puppies do not all develop and grow alike and some grow much faster than others and need more food. The above "menu" need not be altered (except of course that all items are gradually increased) until five months of age, when "tea" can be dropped, and more bread given at midday to compensate. After about four months I cut the meat up into small pieces instead of mincing. With my own Shetland Sheepdogs, I usually give (at five months) two ounces of meat (plus bread) at dinner, and four ounces of meat alone at night, but the amount of the latter depends, of course, on the breed. Plenty of milk is a *sine qua non* for growing puppies, and I give mine breakfast until at least ten months and often longer. Cod liver oil and bone meal should certainly be given till maturity. Yeast tablets (in the concentrated pure form and not with mineral additions which, when bone meal is given, may disturb the delicate balance of mineral intake) are useful, or Vitamin B Complex tablets can be given on veterinary advice. The addition of members of Vit. B Complex help to minimise the possibility of teething fits and are a nerve tonic, but they are not in any way a "cure-all", and puppies properly fed, with brown bread as part of their diet, should not suffer from a deficiency of this group of vitamins. In my kennel, those disorders associated with a deficiency of Vitamin B Complex are mercifully absent.

[1] A baby food which I have found excellent is Familia Swiss Baby Food —an infant form of muesli. It should be mixed with milk a few minutes before giving.

This is perhaps the place to say that I do not use dog biscuits of any kind for rearing puppies, and am also very averse from using dried or tinned meat preparations,[1] especially the former. Whenever possible, raw foods should be given (this does not apply to fish, which must always be cooked) and wholemeal bread, or the cereals I have already mentioned. I am aware that this feeding menu is not a particularly economical one, but this book is not written for the owner of a large commercial kennel, who often is obliged to feed his dogs on the cheapest possible foodstuffs to keep them in reasonably good health. I think very many of the diseases of our times are caused through poor diet—badly balanced—and badly chosen —often consisting of sloppy biscuit meals, and an inadequate supply of meat. A dog is largely what it is fed on; first-class feeding helps to build up his resistance to disease and helps to avoid many troubles such as so-called "eczema", hysteria, etc.

I myself feel that it is not a wise measure to rear puppies by "mass production" methods, as is still done. If there are forty puppies to look after, with or without help, there is little time in which to play with them, to learn to know them and to help them to develop individually. I can speak from experience, having worked in enormous kennels, where a special puppy department (with seldom fewer than thirty puppies) was required. When bitches space out their seasons conveniently, it is usually possible to avoid having more than two or three litters of the same age at one time, and, if necessary, I prefer to wait until a bitch's next season to obviate having too many litters to rear together.

[1] Spratts tinned meat, which is pure meat, cooked in its own juices, with no cereal added, is an exception and I have found it very satisfactory and a most useful stand-by. There are several other good brands of tinned meat which are now available.

CHAPTER XII

WORMING

VETERINARY surgeons are usually strong in their denunciation of the amateur's preoccupation with worming, and in their condemnation of patent vermifuges.

There is no doubt that worming, indulged in so lightly, and usually far too frequently, by the novice, can often cause far more harm than the parasites. Young puppies have died from over-dosing and using strong and drastic "remedies" on a youngster unable to tolerate them. Although very many puppies suffer to a greater or lesser degree from the common round worm, in kennels where strict attention is paid to hygiene, and the dam is clear of the parasites herself, it is unlikely that her offspring will be dangerously affected by these pests. However, it does sometimes happen that even very young puppies—four or five weeks old—suffer a severe set-back owing to the presence of round worms in large numbers. The symptoms—apart from seeing the worms (which are like a thinner and paler edition of the common earth worm) are great thinness, sometimes amounting to emaciation, a generally "tucked up" and unthrifty appearance, variable appetite (sometimes refusing food and sometimes eating greedily), and very often diarrhoea and running eyes. Occasionally the puppy will vomit worms. Unfortunately, little can be done in such cases until the puppy is about seven weeks, but the dangers can be minimised by giving a teaspoonful of olive oil to each puppy every third day.

The choice of a vermifuge must be made with great care.[1] I have tried many advertised preparations at various times, with most disappointing results (most of those I tried were not too drastic, but quite ineffectual), and finally I applied to my veterinary surgeon. That is some years ago now, and I have never regretted my decision; the vermifuge he gives is gentle in its action but remarkably successful, and I can be confident that, if no worms are passed, the puppy is free from them.[2]

A warm day should be chosen for worming, and it is a good idea to vary the puppy's menu slightly the day before, giving the meat meal as the fourth, and adding a teaspoonful of olive oil to it, the final meal being of milk alone. The preparation I use is given in tablet form, which is useful for puppies; it should be given first thing in the morning, followed in an hour by a drink of warm milk. The puppies should, of course, be shut in their kennel for the process. Some three hours after the drink of milk, a light meal of brown bread and milk should be given, and no meat until the evening. The dose should be repeated in five days. With a good vermifuge, the puppies do not seem to be upset by this treatment. Sometimes they need worming again at about three months, and certainly it should be repeated before vaccination against distemper, if there is any reason to think the parasites are present. It is, however, wiser not to worm at all than worm unnecessarily, and the less it is done the better. Much nonsense is talked about the desirability of frequent worming.

While on the subject of frequent dosing, may I add that, with all due deference to the well-known brands,

[1] For garlic as a vermifuge see Chapter XVI.

[2] There are several new preparations available, Piperazine, for example, which are safe, efficient and require no fasting.

condition powders, etc., are never used in my kennel. A dog properly housed, exercised, groomed and fed, should be normally in perfect condition. A sick dog requires veterinary attention as a rule, and *not*, please, treatment with patent remedies, herbal or otherwise. A healthy dog should not need constant dosing to keep him in a state of well-being. It is a curious fact that the less that is known by some novices, the more they feel competent to "diagnose" their animal's ailment, and administer what, to them, seems the appropriate remedy. In many cases, perhaps, if this does no good, it at least does no harm, but in others, where skilled diagnosis and treatment are required, to delay calling in veterinary advice, and to try to treat the disease oneself, may mean the loss of the puppy's life. So, where remedies are suggested in this book, it must be understood that these are mentioned for mild and minor conditions *only*, and where there is any doubt, or any ailment does not quickly disappear, professional advice must be sought.

CHAPTER XIII

EXERCISE AND HOUSING OF YOUNG PUPPIES

At five or six weeks it will be noticed that the puppy is developing some ideas of cleanliness, and, once he can climb out, will relieve himself outside his bed. The bedding will still have to be changed very frequently, however, as "accidents" happen in the best regulated families! In summer, puppies can be put in the open air (provided the weather is warm, with no cold winds) from four and a half weeks onwards. For small breeds, a child's play-pen will be found most useful, as young puppies can be put in this, and it can be moved about. People who own just the one bitch, and are proud of their gardens, should try to make a puppy run, which should be as large as possible. If means permit, a foundation of coarse clinker, topped with a layer of fine gravel or clinker, should be used. This should be very well rolled to form a firm surface. If this is surrounded by a width of grass, the result is ideal for puppies. The gravel or clinker helps in the formation of good feet and the grass is desirable for digging in and amusing themselves generally. The grass should, of course, be kept very short for tiny puppies. Such a surface will drain well, and rarely stay wet for long, even after heavy rain. Concrete or cement, frequently used for runs, is not suitable as, unless extremely well-drained, it is inclined to retain moisture after rain and results in a wet, cold surface. Paths and wide strips of cement in front of kennels are a useful adjunct to kenneling, but the best general surface I have found to be gravel or clinker as described, with cement or concrete in strict moderation. However, the ideal is undoubtedly free range for both puppies and adults, once they grow out of the purely "baby" stage, and, if it is possible to

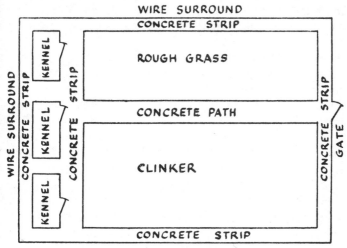

SUGGESTED LAY-OUT OF KENNELS
AND RUN FOR A FEW DOGS

The chain-link surround is set in concrete to prevent digging.

avoid it, I use no runs at all for puppies. Of course, this is only possible in a gentle, non-fighting breed, and where the general lay-out of the garden or kenneling is moderately safe from hazards, such as duck ponds, etc. People are, I find, all too apt to treat puppies as though they were delicate china, and protect them from anything in the way of obstacles in their path, whereas the puppy should learn to avoid them himself, or climb over them.

Very young puppies—say up to six and a half weeks—must be protected in their own interests, and, of course, common sense must be observed, but, broadly speaking, the more natural freedom a puppy gets, once it is out of the early infancy stage, the better. Fresh air and sunshine are excellent, but, if a play-pen is used, it should be put where there is also shade, as very hot sun is not good for youngsters. Puppies reared in natural surroundings, where they have access to earth, grass, rough ground, etc., usually grow up sound and sturdy. Many people make the mistake of not allowing puppies enough exercise and confine them to small runs: in my view, free galloping is essential for every breed and, when so reared, they are far more independent and self-reliant, as they have learnt for themselves how to negotiate obstacles. A small puppy is very unlikely to be injured by being brought up in this way; it is far more probable that they will break their legs or strain a stifle if reared in a small run and not given liberty till six months or over, than if early accustomed to freedom. A young puppy's bones are soft, and he has not far to fall, therefore it is much better for the puppy to learn for himself what he can do. So many youngsters are soft and flabby from lack of exercise. One important point is that they should not be allowed to run up and down stairs at an early age and, similarly, no puppy should be taken for a walk (except a very short one) until six months of age and, in the large breeds, not till older; running about in a reasonably big garden, with opportunities to rest when tired, is quite enough. If the puppy is on its own, it may be necessary to encourage play with a ball or toy, but never let a youngster become over-tired.

It is quite a good plan to carry puppies of the smaller

breeds into the town, into shops, and so forth, as this accustoms them early to strange people and noises. However, strangers should be discouraged from touching the puppy, especially during the teething period (from about four to eight months) as it is all-too-easy to convey infection on the hands. Unless they have been vaccinated, they should not be put on the ground outside the home premises. Apart from training to the lead (in one's garden) walks, as such, should not be indulged in, except for the short excursions mentioned above.

However, we must return to our young puppy of five or six weeks of age. I try to get my own youngsters out into the open air as soon as possible, summer or winter, undeterred even by some light snow on the ground. I think fresh air and exercise are absolutely essential for puppies and, even with winter litters, I have them out as often as weather conditions permit. In other words, I put them out if it is not raining, if it is reasonably dry underfoot (in winter this is sometimes difficult), if there is no *thick* snow, and not a bitter wind. After eight weeks it does not matter so much if the ground is wet but, even so, the puppies should be very carefully dried before putting them back in their kennel, and if they are very likely to get wet underneath, they do not stay out for more than a few minutes at a time. They do, however, make the most of this, and it is very pleasant to see young puppies working off their energies. Damp and cold winds are very bad for them, and wet weather is particularly trying, but I have not found, from experience, that these short games do any harm, provided they are limited, provided it is not actually raining, and provided the ground is not *too* "puddly". It is impossible to expect dry sunny weather in winter, and sunshine is all too often accompanied by frost, and warmth, by rain. In really inclement weather puppies should be put in as large a covered place as possible to romp about—very often, in small kennels or private households, it is the kitchen! And all mats and anything of value at "ground level" should be removed.

With small puppies in play-pens it is a good plan to give them a bed into which they can retire to sleep, as they spend so much time in slumber. Of course this only applies to summer puppies, as the weather would not permit sleeping outdoors in the winter.

The owner of one bitch is unlikely to have a kennel. If the puppies are kept in the kitchen, and he has a good-sized kitchen table, he will find it a wise plan to run fine wire-netting round the legs, and use the enclosed space, otherwise the youngsters will be under everybody's feet as they get active, and be trodden on. Naturally this will be only their living accommodation, as it would be far too restricted for permanent quarters. Of course, in a big house, with a spare room or two, the carpets can be removed, or covered with a thick layer of newspaper. Or, if a play-pen is used, this can be placed in the room, on a square of linoleum, first covered thickly by sawdust, and then newspaper. It is very important to keep either kennel or kennel substitute scrupulously clean and one can hardly err on the side of being too thorough and fussy in this respect. Kennels should be scrubbed regularly and cleaned out at least once a day and more often in bad weather. Dry sawdust forms the best floor covering and, when cleaning, remove the soiled parts, wipe the places with a good diluted efficient disinfectant, and, finally, sprinkle fresh sawdust liberally. Sawdust is the most pleasant and hygienic of all absorbent materials which I have used; peat, while antiseptic, is unsatisfactory, as it makes the dogs' coats very dirty, and newspaper is a most inadequate substitute for sawdust. It is a good plan to treat all kennel floors with linseed oil and varnish, as suggested for sleeping-boxes. Properly cleaned and cared-for kennels should not smell in the least. The fact that they all-too-often do so, reflects no credit on owner or kennelmaid.

Puppies should not be fed near, or on sawdust, hay or woodwool. If any of these substances get into their food the consequences may be very serious.

CHAPTER XIV

HANDLING AND TRAINING HINTS

I DO not propose, in this book, to give full details on training puppies, as this has so often been done before by far more able pens than mine. However, a few hints may be helpful.

"House manners", perhaps the first and most important lesson for a puppy, and the one whose mastery is the most desired by the new owner, cannot be acquired by a very young puppy, and it is not fair to expect this. But, from the age of about ten weeks, rudimentary rules of behaviour can be learnt and, often with surprising speed, the puppy becomes house-trained. In some breeds this is learnt more easily than in others, and there is no doubt that a puppy bred from house-trained parents has a natural inclination towards cleanliness.

A youngster should always be placed outside directly he wakes from sleep, immediately after a rowdy game, and also after food. But do not expect him to "last" through the night; he will do his best, but there will certainly be some "puddles" to begin with, even if he is let out last thing at night and early in the morning. In a long spell of bad weather, when it is impossible to put the puppy out, he should be trained to use a large shallow box partly filled with sawdust. When an "accident" happens, if you are there at the time, say "No" very firmly, and put the puppy out at once. Never smack him, he will not understand your objection to a perfectly natural function. And do not indulge in the cruel and useless practice of rubbing the puppy's nose in it. If you can "catch" him in the act of relieving himself, so much the better; picked up immediately, with obvious disapproval in your voice, and placed outside, he will very quickly learn that his behaviour is "not done", and will try to restrain himself but, I must repeat, do not expect too much. Never, never lose your temper with a puppy, however exasperating he is, and never smack him. If he persistently behaves badly, it is usually due to some fault in his training and he is rarely to blame. The word "No!" accompanied by a growl, is usually quite enough. He can also be taught not to jump up or get on chairs by the same methods— firmness, patience, and consistency. It is no use saying "No" to a puppy one minute, and then ignoring him the next because you are too busy to attend to him.

Training to the lead can be begun any time after three months. I use a very small, light collar and allow the puppy to get accustomed to the "feel" of that before I attach a lead. Then, when he has stopped scratching and shaking to get it off, I attach a light lead, and let him run about with it loose and trailing. When he is used to that, I pick up the end, and let him go where he will, while I follow; if this is not done, and I tried to pull on the lead, ten to one the puppy would sit down, look mutinous and refuse to move. The next step is to try and persuade him to walk the way *I* want (not always easy!) by calling him, presenting him with tit-bits, and so on. Puppies differ very much in the speed with which they become lead-trained, some taking longer than others, but, however long it takes, and however exasperated you get with your pupil, do not show it, and try to keep your patience and your temper. It is not wise to take him on roads where there is traffic until he is thoroughly accustomed to the lead and has been "schooled" in walking on quiet roads and lanes.

When the puppy is completely used to the lead, do not allow him to pull—have him on a short leash and "check" him from going ahead, saying "Heel" and pulling him back, his head level with your knee. Always have him on your left. He should be taught, as far as possible, to ignore strange dogs, and to behave himself both in and out of shops and on the public pavement. No dog should be allowed to relieve himself where he likes, but should be trained to use the gutter. A well-behaved dog is a pleasure to take out, but one which tugs on his lead, fights with every dog he sees, and relieves himself on merchandise both in and out of shops, gives plenty of "ammunition" to the "dog-haters". However well trained the animal, he should be kept on the lead in shops, as some people are nervous of dogs, and one "at large" is looked at askance by non dog-lovers.

If you take your dog with you into a restaurant, keep him in an unobtrusive position, and not where he will trip up every waitress, and do not commit the cardinal crime of letting him have your plate to lick! Do not let him sit on chairs or seats in public places, and, if you take him by train, have him on your lap if small enough or, if you *must* have him on the seat (and many railway officials object strongly to this) first put newspaper or a coat for him to sit on. This is a dog-loving country, but there are quite a number of people who rather dislike dogs, and while we do not agree with them, they have a right to our consideration, and I can imagine nothing worse for the confirmed "dog-hater" than a very obtrusive puppy, all over the seat of a public vehicle, and jumping up on the other passengers.

Insist on obedience; a puppy must come when it is called, but it is no use punishing it for not doing so, until it understands what you mean. Reward it and praise it highly when it comes in answer to your call. Never shout at a puppy—you will only cow it.

Be careful in your handling of a youngster and, if you have children, insist that they are careful too, and teach them the proper way. When picking up a puppy, put one hand under its chest, being careful to have its front legs enclosed *in* your hand and arm, and do not allow the elbows to stick out at right angles. All too many puppies become "out at elbow" when adult if these precautions are not observed. A small puppy's hindquarters can be supported against your body, but a big and heavy one should have its hindquarters supported with your other hand. Do not be too ready to pick up youngsters by the scruff of the neck—it can be abused, especially by children. Remember, puppies are very "wriggly" little things, so hold them firmly in case they jump out of your arms.

Long-haired breeds should never wear a collar, except when out (the "rolled" kind is the best) and a harness for any breed is very undesirable, as it ruins the coat and shoulders.

Toys for puppies—apart from the ever-popular carpet slipper—can consist of stiff envelopes tied tightly in the middle, old stockings knotted in the middle, and the like. Rubber bones and rubber toys generally are highly dangerous because of the risk of swallowing bits of them. Many operations are performed for the removal of these "foreign bodies". This is perhaps the place to say that I have never yet met a veterinary surgeon who approved of bones being given to dogs and puppies. As they seem to spend so much of their time in dealing with the harmful results thereof, perhaps it is not surprising. If you feel you *must* give your puppy something of that kind, only marrow bones should be used, and be sure these are smooth, with no loose, jagged bits attached. Rabbit and poultry bones are extremely dangerous and should never be given.

CHAPTER XV

Puppies should have their skins examined from time to time as, during the summer, especially if other livestock is kept, there is a danger of lice and fleas. Fleas are fairly easily seen, and the black, dust-like excreta left in their wake is a certain sign that these pests are present. Lice are not so easy to detect, unless they have been present for some time, when there will be obvious incessant irritation and eczema-like sores, caused by the scratching. The places most favoured by lice are in the folds and creases of the skin—behind the ears, under the chin, in the arm-pits, and so on. If they are not very numerous they can be removed with a pair of forceps and either dropped in paraffin or burnt. B.H.C. (Gammexane) is a safe modern insecticide. Preparations containing D.D.T. should never be used on puppies as they can be very dangerous particularly with the very young. When using any powder of this kind, care must be taken to protect the puppy's eyes, or they may become inflamed and irritated. The dusting with powder should be repeated in three to five days, and possibly a third time. It will usually be found that lice attack a delicate puppy rather than the strong ones; indeed, it is possible to have only one puppy affected in a litter.

Skin troubles should not be common in puppies which are properly cared for. Incidentally, any puppy with signs of this should be examined carefully to make sure he is not suffering from the external parasites mentioned above, as it is astonishing how many owners are not aware their pets have lice and fleas.

In very hot weather puppies may develop bare patches under their chins or elsewhere, often at teething time or just before; sometimes these are due to diet, but often it corresponds to "heat-rash" in human babies. The patches are mildly irritating, but there is little or no inflammation, and they disappear, as a rule, without treatment. Dermatitis of the "eczematous" variety is rare in puppies properly reared and given sufficient meat, and it will usually be found to yield to simple treatment with castor oil and zinc ointment in the dry form or, (in the pustular variety) to Calamine (Veterinary). Iodine Oil is often very successful with both forms, and it is also most useful for those bare patches which sometimes occur with no obvious skin trouble.[1] Some types of dry "scurfy" dermatitis owe their origin to insufficient fat in the diet, and in these cases olive oil or cod liver oil, and a certain proportion of fatty meat, should be given daily with the food.

It is not always easy for even the experienced owner to differentiate between what is usually, but rather incorrectly, called "eczema" and the various forms of parasitic skin trouble loosely called "mange". The latter takes so many forms, sometimes so baffling for the veterinary surgeon as well as the owner, that it is not possible to describe the likely symptoms except to say that, in the most common type, the first parts usually attacked are the chest, arm-pits, elbows, hock-joints and round the eyes. The eruptions (in the initial stage) resemble flea-bites, and are not easily seen. There are many well-tried remedies for this form of mange (known as sarcoptic), sulphur ointment and Gammexane being amongst the

[1] Calamine (Veterinary) and Iodine Oil are both products of Crookes Laboratories.

most useful; another remedy, benzyl benzoate, should only be used under veterinary supervision as it is a highly dangerous drug, and is sometimes not so efficacious as the older remedies, although much pleasanter to use. It must be remembered that mange is contagious, and although there seems to be some doubt whether this also applies to the variety known as demodectic or follicular, it is wiser to treat it as such. Isolation should be rigid, and disinfection very thorough, as re-infection is common. All cases of suspected mange should be seen by a veterinary surgeon, and the same applies to persistent dermatitis of a non-infectious origin. Diet must receive special attention.

Occasionally horse-meat will be found to have an over-heating effect, especially in hot weather, and it can then be substituted by fish, eggs, tripe, etc. Starch should be reduced, and a little green vegetable given daily. Most forms of skin trouble of this kind are a sign that all is not well with the body, and the toxins are erupted in this way; it is useless, therefore, to treat the trouble simply by external applications without eliminating the cause. Some forms of dermatitis are hereditary, which make it all the more important for healthy breeding stock to be chosen. In a puppy with a very tender and hyper-sensitive skin, irritation or mild inflammation can be caused by hard and "prickly" bedding, insect powders, and from overcrowding and stuffy sleeping quarters, etc. The presence of worms in large numbers occasionally causes a slight pustular eruption on abdomen and thighs, which rather resembles the eruption sometimes seen in young distemper subjects. The latter is, however, accompanied by very obvious illness. Skin troubles, their source, diagnosis and treatment, are opening up a very wide field for research. It is at least possible that some baffling forms of dermatitis are due to psychopathic causes (as is often the case with humans) or by allergic conditions.

Puppies should be groomed daily from the age of three months. Newspapers will be found extremely useful for drying purposes as they are very absorbent and remove the mud in a minute. From a trial of both methods I am convinced that newspaper is far superior to either towels or wash-leather. I never use sawdust for drying dogs, as it is possible that a dog with a hyper-sensitive skin might be adversely affected by its use and, in any case, I do not find it satisfactory for this purpose.

Running eyes are a frequent and very annoying trouble. Again the cause must be found, if possible, and the eyes carefully examined. Sometimes worms are the reason, or even a cold wind. In other cases there may be some abnormality present, for example, entropion (turned-in eyelids, which mean the lashes irritate the delicate corneal surface), ectropion (where the lids turn outwards), or odd extra eyelashes growing inside the ordinary rows, and having the same effect as entropion. The latter unpleasant condition can be cured by operation (and this must be performed by a really first-class surgeon), but the only way to deal with the odd eye-lash problem is to extract the offending eyelashes with fine forceps. This must be done with the greatest care and, unless the owner is very experienced, has a steady hand—and a quiet dog!—it is better carried out by a veterinarian, who will use a local anaesthetic. The lashes grow again, but if they are removed every two or three months, the eye can be kept clear. Some puppies have very small eyes, and have a way of blinking and screwing up their eyelids in bright sun, but, unfortunately, there is no remedy for this condition.

Ordinary cases of watering (with, or without mattery discharge) should be dealt with by dropping in castor oil two or three times a day and using golden eye ointment at night. If due to local infection (as is often the case) penicillin eye ointment is invaluable. There are so many forms of eye trouble that if persistent, in spite of treatment, veterinary advice should be obtained. For washing out the eye, use warm boracic lotion (a teaspoonful of the crystals to a pint of water). In summer, puppies sometimes get grass seeds or other "foreign bodies" into their eyes, and any case of acute ophthalmic trouble should be carefully investigated. The grass seeds cannot always be seen, and can cause blindness if not removed without delay. Diarrhoea is a common puppy trouble. The causes are legion, and it should be regarded as a symptom and not as an illness in itself. Like dermatitis, it is useless to treat the disorder without finding what lies behind it. As it is a common symptom of both "hard pad" and distemper, the temperature should be taken when the puppy has been resting; the normal is from 38–38·5°C. (100·6–101·5°F.), but a puppy tends to run a higher temperature than an adult so, for practical purposes, one can take anything over 38·8°C. (102·2°F.) as indicative of fever. Any temporary derangement can cause a slight temperature, but if the thermometer records 39°C. (102·5°F.) or over, it is a warning sign. Take the temperature again an hour later, and, if it is still up, report to your veterinarian. It is much better for you to have to pay for a (perhaps unnecessary) visit than have a very much bigger bill for a neglected "hard pad" case.

Even if the temperature is normal the puppy should be isolated, and his temperature taken twice daily for two or three days as a precautionary measure. The diet of diarrhoea cases needs careful attention, and arrowroot, cornflour and rather stodgy food should be given. A *small dose* of castor oil may be given initially if there is no fever, but if the diarrhoea does not yield to treatment reasonably quickly, veterinary assistance should be sought. Although it may easily be due to some dietetic indiscretion, worms, etc., it is so often associated with the virus diseases that it can be a very ominous symptom. Experiments with medicines are not advisable, and bismuth, chlorodyne and glucose should be given only with veterinary approval. Diarrhoea caused by harmful bacteria has its appropriate remedy in a "sulpha" drug acting directly on the intestines, and kaolin and chlorodyne may be required for other types. Diarrhoea is often caused by faulty hygiene in kennel or run, by too much, or unsuitable food, by inferior biscuit meals, by food which is slightly tainted, and by worms. Puppies with the trouble should be isolated, their excreta carefully removed, and disinfectant used liberally, as apart from the risk of the virus diseases, many troubles of this type are infectious.

Dogs with long ears (such as Spaniels and Setters) should have the inside of the ears examined from time to time. Otitis externa ("canker") which looks like brown dirt in the ears, should be treated by cleaning out the ear *gently* (with no "prodding") with cotton wool wrapped around forceps; Calamine lotion can be used for this. There are many remedies for the trouble; with simple, uncomplicated cases, where there is also acute irritation of the ear flap, castor oil and zinc ointment is often effective, so too is Crooke's Calamine lotion (Veterinary). Ottorrhoea (where the discharge from the ear is purulent and evil-smelling) should be dealt with by the veterinary surgeon. Penicillin ointment is remarkably effective in many cases. This should not be regarded as a minor ailment as abscesses can be caused, and the dog become deaf for life by neglect or using harmful or unsuitable remedies.

Simple wounds should have the hair removed round the lesion and be bathed in the appropriate solution of Dettol. A puppy which limps may have a thorn in its paw; the thorn should be removed with fine forceps and the puncture dabbed with iodine.

In snowy weather it is a good idea to rub vaseline freely between the toes and pads, as it prevents the snow "balling" there. This particularly applies to Cocker Spaniels, which can suffer from a painful local inflammatory dermatitis between the toes from this cause.

Interdigital cysts are painful swellings between the toes in breeds such as Sealyhams; they should be treated by a veterinary surgeon, as acute pain and much harm can be caused by painting them with tincture of iodine (or other counter-irritant) at the wrong moment.

Coughs and "colds" should never be neglected. A simple "cold" (unaccompanied by fever) usually clears up quickly by holding the puppy's head over a basin of Friar's Balsam and boiling water and making him inhale the vapour. Coughs are a symptom—possibly of distemper —and are unusual in puppies. While glycerine in small doses will often give relief, this is a matter for a veterinary surgeon, as coughs are so often due to "hard pad" or distemper.

CHAPTER XVI

DISTEMPER, "HARD PAD" AND VIRAL HEPATITIS: IMMUNISATION AND PREVENTION

I WOULD like to repeat, at the beginning of this chapter, what I have said before—that so many cases of illness believed, by the owner, to be minor, eventually prove to be "hard pad" or distemper, and the start of the former is often very insidious. It is therefore far better to inform your veterinary surgeon, and perhaps call him in unnecessarily, than for an animal starting a virus disease not to receive early treatment, which sometimes means the difference between ultimate recovery or the reverse.

When reporting to a veterinary surgeon, if the case is complicated, it is wiser to write down the details beforehand, so that nothing is forgotten. If you wish him to visit your dog, 'phone him early in the day, and try to avoid calling him in at the week-end or at holiday times. Reports should be concise, and confined to facts, so that the practitioner is not forced to extract the essentials from a mass of irrelevant data. Febrile temperature (if any), diarrhoea or vomiting, appetite (whether good or the reverse), coughing, any signs of pain or distress, and the dog's general appearance (whether bright or depressed) are all facts which will help the veterinary surgeon to decide whether the case sounds serious or not. If a visit is to be made, have everything ready beforehand to save a busy practitioner's time—a steady table covered with an old sheet and newspaper for use in examining the puppy, Dettol, cotton wool, one or two empty dishes for soiled swabs, etc. A *sine qua non* is a good light, whether natural or artificial. The puppy should be firmly held while being examined. Remember, it is the veterinary surgeon's business to make a diagnosis so, when giving a history of the case, or making any other comments, refrain from giving your own (probably incorrect) interpretation of the significance of symptoms and behaviour. Listen carefully to instructions (if necessary writing them down) and if there is something you do not understand, ask for explanation and repetition; it is much better to be thought stupid than to endanger your puppy's life by forgetting or misunderstanding instructions. For serious illnesses a "case history" should be kept in diary form.

This is not a book on nursing, so I will not refer to this more than to say that much the same qualities are needed for this as for whelping—close observation (this is vital in many diseases such as "hard pad"), gentleness, avoidance of "fuss" and keeping the patient as quiet as possible. Many devoted owners will not allow a sick animal to rest quietly, as they are continually going in to see how the dog is or to pet him; all patients need rest, quiet and sleep, especially in cases where the nervous system is likely to be affected, and, for this reason, all cases of serious illness should be nursed away from noise, whether human or canine, whether infectious or not. A kitchen, with its endless bustle, is not at all a suitable place. The quarters should be quiet, warm and airy, and, in winter, there will have to be artificial heating—but there should always be ventilation. Remember to pay scrupulous attention to hygiene, especially when there is diarrhoea (which should be removed, as far as possible, as soon as it occurs) and the discharge from eyes and nose should be removed frequently in diseases (such as distemper) where it is profuse. A little vaseline should be applied to the nostrils afterwards. Large tea-chests with wire fronts make useful "sick wards" for dogs seriously ill, as it is possible to have several in the same room, and they

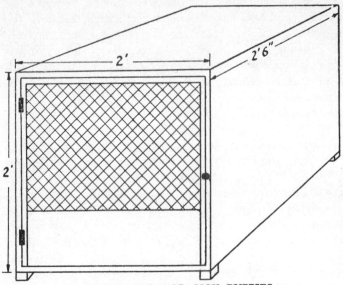

A USEFUL BED FOR SICK PUPPIES

This can be made to any size. The above is suitable for small and medium sized breeds. A smaller bed can be placed inside.

are kept quiet and warm and out of draughts. The drugs, and any special diet ordered, will be the veterinary surgeon's province, and the nursing will be done under his supervision.

Distemper is, of course, much dreaded by dog owners, and its close cousin "hard pad" (the more dangerous of the two) is an ever-present bogy. Puppies should not be handled by strangers or allowed to go out of house and garden until they have been immunised against distemper. It is asking for trouble to take a young puppy into the street, allowing him to mix with other dogs, and the same applies to taking him to a veterinary surgery or clinic. The best natural protection against both distemper and "hard pad" is perfect health and rearing—a sickly, badly reared puppy or one brought up in very artificial "hot-house" conditions, has little stamina or resistance to disease, and is likely to succumb if he becomes infected. When "below par" for any reason, as when badly affected by worms, or during the teething period, a puppy is far more likely to pick up infection. Vaccination should not be regarded as a substitute for the natural protectionof good rearing and sound health, but as an additional precaution.

Both distemper and "hard pad" have rather similar initial symptoms, and it is often difficult for even a veterinary surgeon to differentiate between the two in the early stages, but both diseases need immediate skilled attention, and it is very dangerous to delay and still more to give proprietary remedies. "Hard pad", in particular, is often an extremely fatal disease, and appears in very different forms; sometimes, with the best skill in the world, the mortality rate is heavy, but prompt attention at least reduces the risk, and gives the patient every chance.

The symptoms of distemper are well known, but do not always follow the pattern of the text-book—sometimes the preliminary stage is not very marked, and not all distemper patients have running nose, eyes, etc. In all the cases I have noticed, however, there has been great listlessness, heaviness and sleepiness to begin with. A puppy which lies about, goes into corners, is seen to be shivering and looks dull and listless, should have its temperature taken. Distemper is sometimes a sudden disease, and in one outbreak, a dog which was well to all intents and purposes (normal temperature, cheerful and good appetite) in the morning, had a temperature of 40·5°C. (105°F.) at night, and had the symptoms mentioned above. There may or may not be discharge from the eyes at this stage; the nose is usually dry. There is commonly complete loss of appetite and often tonsilitis and diarrhoea. The initial temperature is usually high, but not invariably so. Some of the worst horrors of distemper have been removed or alleviated by the discovery of the modern antibiotics (penicillin and the like) and new drugs are constantly being brought into use. Curiously enough, while the "sulpha" group of drugs are often very successful in distemper, they are definitely contra-indicated in "hard pad". It is possible to get distemper twice, so no dog can really be considered to be "over distemper". The presence of marked teeth usually means that a dog has had distemper, but it is not invariably the case, as deficiency of calcium at teething time can also cause this.

Since this book was first written, much has been done in the field of immunisation against the most serious canine diseases, the distemper virus complex (of which "hard pad" is a member) viral hepatitis (H.C.C.) and the leptospiral diseases, leptospiral canicola and leptospiral icterohaemorrhagia.

Today, combined vaccines are available to immunise the puppy against these diseases with the minimum amount of fuss and separate injections. Not only have these immunising procedures been "streamlined" but, as a result of new and advanced methods of manufacture, the vaccines are today more efficient and reliable than they have ever been. Added to the improvements in the manufacture of these vaccines, is the newer "measles vaccine", which, owing to the similarity of the measles virus of humans and the distemper virus of dogs, a vaccine prepared from the measles virus can now be used in very young puppies to protect them temporarily against distemper virus. It should be emphasised that the measles vaccine is not a replacement of the traditional distemper vaccination process, but an addition of value in certain special cases and as with the immunising processes of all these vaccines discussed here, your veterinary surgeon is best equipped to advise you which one to use, either as a routine prevention or under special circumstances as an outbreak of distemper in your neighbourhood. Fortunately as more dogs are immunised, the risk of epidemics of distemper, as used to happen, is reduced. In fact, with the full co-operation of the dog owners of this country, the eradication of distemper—the dreaded and feared disease of dogs for centuries—would be a practical proposition. Let us hope that in the years to come distemper will only be a disease read about in books, and never experienced as an epidemic disease in the United Kingdom.

Hepatitis, referred to earlier, is another serious virus disease to which, unfortunately, puppies seem particularly susceptible. First identified by a Swede (Rubarth), this disease has been common in America for many years, but although no doubt existing here for a considerable time, its widespread nature and gravity have only recently been recognised. As viral hepatitis takes many forms, it is extremely difficult to diagnose, often being confused with distemper, and as it can kill a dog in a few hours its existence may only be discovered on post-mortem. Although the deaths in contagious hepatitis are not very high, it can have very far-reaching effects. A dog which has recovered can act as a "carrier" for many months and infect others, and dams which have had the disease can infect their unborn puppies, with the result that the whole littter can die at a few days old. If a recovered dog contracts distemper or "hard pad" (or even a milder complaint) it can do so in a very serious and virulent form, and many cases of acute "hard pad", on being post-mortemed, have been found to be carrying hepatitis virus. The virus attacks the liver, often causing permanent damage, and the disease can exist unrecognised until a dog is found dead one morning though apparently all right the night before. Although dogs of any age can be affected, puppies and youngsters are the most susceptible, particularly while resistance is lowered as during teething. Although the dog can have the disease without any apparent symptoms except perhaps lassitude and slight depression for a few hours, the usual symptoms in a sub-acute case are: fever (103–104.6°F.), depression, inappetance, sometimes abdominal pain and tonsilitis; sometimes vomiting and discharge from the eyes. Depression is always present, and if it persists and deepens the outlook is bad. The course of the disease is short—a week or ten days—and recovery takes place with a gradual drop in temperature and a return to good spirits. Alternatively, the animal may become more and more depressed, refuse all food, vomit frequently, suffer acutely from thirst, and collapse with jaundice and internal haemorrhage. As there is often great abdominal pain in addition, the final stages of this form are very distressing. With acute viral hepatitis death occurs in a few hours, usually accompanied by a very high temperature, fits and coma. Gamma-globulin or specific antisera may be used in the treatment of this acute virus disease or, more important, in the protection of in-contacts in the litter or kennels. Treatment must, of course, be left to the veterinary surgeon, but absolute quiet, warmth, and lots of glucose are essential in nursing.

Although contagious (by direct contact), viral hepatitis is not so readily conveyed as some other virus diseases, and many dogs—perhaps the majority—have it so mildly that it is unnoticeable. Vaccines are now effective in immunising puppies against this virus and these are available in two main forms, as a live, attenuated form or as a dead vaccine, that is where the virus has been inactivated completely prior to its injection into the dog. Your veterinary surgeon will advise you on the best one to use in your own particular circumstances.

Some breeders disapprove very much of any form of injection. They have, of course, a perfect right to their own opinion, and it is true that some dogs appear to have a natural immunity to disease and can be exposed to infection without harm. A perfectly healthy dog, well-fed and well-reared, already has a certain amount of natural resistance, and I prefer to add to this by giving him, in addition, the protections devised by modern science. Nevertheless, should it ever become impossible for me to have my own dogs vaccinated, I would rely *alone* on the resistance of good health, and not give them patent medicines of any kind to prevent infection. This is only a personal feeling, and I must admit that I have not tried garlic (for which many claims are made in this respect) for this purpose, but I have never yet met a veterinary surgeon who had any confidence in it.

During the 1918 influenza epidemic, the medical profession tried all sorts of drugs in an effort to check the menace, and my father (a medical practitioner) tried garlic among other things, but although every extravagant claim possible was made for its wonderful powers, both curative and preventative, it had no effect whatsoever. I did, however, many years ago, try garlic as a preventative and cure for round worms in puppies, and again I am merely voicing a personal experience when I say that I found it absolutely useless—indeed, worse than useless.

In actual practice, I have found that a well-reared puppy, bred from a healthy well-fed dam, and reared in hygienic surroundings, with plenty of fresh air and sunlight, is unlikely to have much trouble with worms. It is not natural, in my view, for a healthy puppy to be heavily infested and, if he is, there is probably something wrong about his upbringing. I remember, pre-war, my veterinary surgeon post-mortemed a ten-week puppy of mine (which had died of leptospiral jaundice) and told me there were no worms present at all, although that particular litter had not been wormed owing to severe weather.

As a final remark on immunisation, the best age for this is at ten to twelve weeks of age. If puppies are inoculated at a younger age, the presence of maternal antibodies may interfere with immunisation, so, if inoculation for some reason is desirable then, the puppy should be given a further booster injection at five months of age. This should on no account be neglected as there is a serious risk of the puppy contracting "hard pad" or distemper if this is not done. No method of immunisation is permanent so it is a wise precaution to give dogs "booster" doses every eighteen months to two years, particularly if there is a local outbreak of these diseases or if the dog has not come into contact with any infection while protected with the original inoculation.

CHAPTER XVII

TEETHING AND SIMPLE MEDICINES

FROM about four to four-and-a-half months, the puppy will be engaged in changing his teeth to the permanent set. The process is usually completed by seven or eight months, but some puppies take longer than others. It is necessary to examine the mouth from time to time to make sure all the milk teeth are dropping out as the permanent ones come through, as if they are not shed simultaneously with the eruption of the others, the permanent teeth may become crooked or displaced. This applies particularly to the "canines" (those big tusk-like teeth) and if the milk teeth do not come out reasonably quickly (they should be loosened by gently "working" them from time to time) they should be extracted.

Although most puppies show no physical signs of teething at all, there are occasional cases of teething upsets, which vary from very real, though slight malaise, to disinclination to eat when the gums are painful. If (by examining the mouth) it appears the latter is the case, give the food soft and warm—some persuasion may be necessary. Teething fits are a very common phenomenon, although I have had very little trouble with these; the puppy rushes about madly, screaming and knocking into things. Members of Vitamin B Complex help to prevent these disorders. Chloretone[1] is a safe remedy on such occasions, and a light diet (milk predominating) should be given for forty-eight hours following an attack. The puppy should be kept as quiet as possible, and not allowed

[1] See footnote, page 45.

to play in the hot sun. The teething process is, however, a natural one, and, normally, there is no derangement at all.

I have said before, and I reiterate here, that it is a mistake to be dosing puppies constantly. A healthy youngster does not need this. Incidentally, I have never found that green vegetable added to the diet is at all necessary, provided the dogs have access to grass and otherherbage, which they usually eat freely. For town dogs, I think it advisable. I often give my puppies a whole carrot to chew like a bone, and they thoroughly enjoy this.

Constipation should be very unusual, given a balanced diet with wholemeal and "roughage" and plenty of exercise, but if a laxative is required, olive oil is safe, and as it is also a food, the excess is readily absorbed. Liquid paraffin is a mineral, and as it clogs the absorption mechanism of the intestines and may actually be harmful, it is better avoided. Castor oil—which is a purgative and not a laxative—should never be used for this purpose.

Aspirin is very useful for minor aches and pains and is often advised by the veterinary surgeon. It has the disadvantage of usually making the animal sick, but in recent years a new soluble preparation has been evolved which, so far, has never caused vomiting with my own dogs, although they cannot tolerate the ordinary kind: I refer to "Disprin" brand.

Glucose is a most useful stand-by and forms easily digested nourishment and is also mildly stimulating. It is very effective in cases of shock.

For a dog seriously ill, particularly when vomiting, the following will be found excellent (subject to veterinary approval): half a pint of milk, two or three teaspoonfuls of brandy, one to two egg-whites, and a tablespoonful of glucose; the mixture to be given frequently in teaspoonful "doses". A variant, useful for nephritis (kidney) cases is : half a pint of skimmed milk, tablespoonful of glucose, teaspoonful of brandy, two egg-whites and two tablespoonfuls of

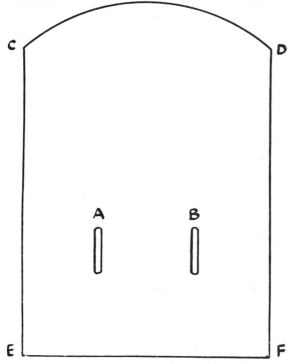

PATTERN FOR PNEUMONIA JACKET

The puppy's front legs are put through the holes A and B. Stitch E to F behind his neck and continue down the back till C meets D. Never use safety pins.

barley water. A safe and excellent tonic, should one ever be necessary, is Collovet (Crookes) obtainable from one's veterinary surgeon.

A puppy with any signs of a cough should be put, as a precautionary measure, in a pneumonia jacket, made very simply from a piece of blanket, into which two holes (to take the forelegs) are made. There should be sufficient material allowed in front of the holes for the coat to be drawn well up the front of the chest. Put the puppy's legs through the holes, draw up the front part, and the portion round his "tummy" and sew him into it. The part coming under the body should extend midway down to cover his lungs. A tape sewn to each side of the neck will help to keep it tidy.

CHAPTER XVIII

EXHIBITING PUPPIES

LET me say at the outset that we must face the fact
that showing puppies is a very risky business, especially
at the big winter championship shows, and if we wish
to be sure not only of giving the puppy reasonable
protection but also of preventing infection being carried
to the dogs at home, many precautions (some of them
rather tiresome) will have to be taken. Some exhibitors
cannot be bothered to take even sensible measures, and
prefer to risk trouble rather than exert themselves in any
way, but this seems, to put it mildly, rather a short-
sighted attitude in view of the severity of some of the
prevalent diseases. When whole litters of promising
puppies can be wiped out by carelessness (to use no
stronger word) it is surely worth while going to a little
trouble.

For most of us shows are a necessary evil, and if
we have a promising puppy we want to show it. I think
we must remember, however, that apart from the risk
of infection there is such a thing as showing a puppy
too much. The period of growth and development is not
long in dogs, and every minute of it is occupied in this.
Exhibiting from time to time is unlikely to do harm to a
healthy youngster, but to take a puppy from show to
show, with only a few days (if that) in between, during a
period of months, is a very different matter. They have
no chance to recover from the fatigue and nerve-strain
of one show before they are rushed to another, often

with a long journey involved. Such exhibitors must themselves be very strong! and, in their determination to win challenge certificates (it is usually a "budding champion" which is subjected to this kind of treatment) they are blind to the possible effect on the puppy. Some youngsters seem to enjoy shows, but many dislike them, even if the fact is not very obvious, and their physical reaction is eloquent testimony. Usually these "show sick" puppies become very thin, even emaciated and, even if they show well to start with, begin to show badly, become distracted and, quite obviously, have had enough of the whole business. The strain of a big show is very considerable, even under the most comfortable conditions, and we all know that, however pleasant we try to make the travelling, and so on, it is not always possible to ensure comfort in crowded railway carriages. Of course, it is quite different to show a puppy *reasonably* often, but do not over-do it; remember, a dog's adolescence is short, and he should utilise the period to the full. Show conditions are never natural and are the reverse of healthy!

No puppy which is not in perfect health should be shown as, if below par, there is a far greater susceptibility to other infections, often prevalent at a show.

If he is small enough it is wiser to carry him, when arriving at the show, until well past the crowd of exhibitors and dogs at the entrance. The show bench should be thoroughly disinfected before putting the puppy on it. If there is any straw, it should be removed, and several layers of newspaper put down, with a blanket on top, which will well cover the "floor" of the bench. Netting should be hung over the front (the kind sold for gardens is quite suitable) as this prevents the puppy being touched by the "gate" and allows him to rest undisturbed. If it is possible to avoid it, the puppy should not be exercised at the show, as the ground set aside for this purpose at indoor shows is a fruitful source of infection of all kinds. Keep him on the bench. Provided he is given a good run

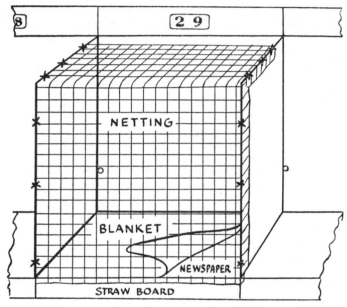

A SHOW BENCH PREPARED FOR A PUPPY

The netting is fastened by bulldog clips at the points marked with crosses.

immediately before going to the show, he should be comfortable enough, unless a journey is involved, when it is usually possible to exercise him before going in. Raw meat should be taken as food—it is concentrated and not bulky. I do not disinfect my puppy at the show as he at once becomes re-infected, so I prefer to do this thoroughly at home.

There is some risk attached to showing dogs, especially puppies, and there is an infectious enteritis which is fairly common after some of the big winter shows. This is annoying but not often dangerous; however, it is extremely infectious and spreads like wildfire to all the other kennel inmates. Sometimes there is a slight temperature but often the only symptoms are lack of appetite, sometimes vomiting, and diarrhoea. The veterinary surgeon should be consulted to ensure that the malady is not anything more serious, but although a tiresome complaint which can materially affect the condition of puppies between the age of five and seven months, it does not usually last very long. Modern methods of immunisation have made the old dangers attached to dog shows much less frequent.

"DO'S AND DON'TS"

DO see the puppy has regular times for sleeping—so important for young things.

DO talk to puppies and play with them as often as you can.

DO keep your puppies under constant observation—many an illness can be nipped in the bud in this way.

DO remember that a puppy's natural condition should be that of health—and he does not need drugs or "conditioners" to maintain this.

DO be gentle in your handling of a puppy, and insist on others being the same. Many puppies have been made nervous for life by unintentionally rough treatment.

DON'T give patent medicines of any kind, nor consult your local chemist nor the nearest dog breeder in preference to a good veterinary surgeon.

DON'T forget to have a clinical thermometer (the half-minute human kind is best) in the house and USE IT if in doubt.

DON'T expect too much from your puppy when training him.

DON'T lose your temper or your patience—the latter quality is quite essential for puppy-rearing.

DON'T let your puppy become a nuisance to other people.

ADDENDUM

Litter Recording:
    If no dogs in litter registered at the time of recording litter £5.00 plus £1.00 for each puppy in the litter
    If one or more dogs in litter registered at time of recording litter £5.00 per puppy named plus £1.00 for each puppy not named in the litter
Registration (per dog) £5.00
Registration in Obedience Record £5.00
Endorsement Name Unchangeable (additional fee) £5.00
Re-registration £5.00
Transfer £5.00
Loan or use of bitch £5.00
Change of name £5.00
Pedigrees—3 generations £6.00
Pedigrees—Export £20.00
List of Wins (entered in Stud Book) £0.57
Registration of Affix £10.00
Affix Maintenance Fee (Annual) £5.00
Assumed Name £5.00
Registration of Title £5.75
Maintenance of Title £5.75
Formation of a Branch by a Registered Society £3.45
Maintenance of Title of a Branch of a Registered Society £3.45
Registration of Title of Dog Training Club £5.75
Maintenance of Title of Dog Training Club £5.75
For Shows held under Kennel Club Show Rules:
    Licence to hold a General and Group Championship Show £23.00
    Licence to hold a Championship Show £11.50
    Licence to hold an Open Show £5.75

Licence to hold a Limited or Sanction Show £2.87

The following Extra Fees are payable for Championship and
Open Shows:

For each 500 exhibits (or part) £2.30

For permission to hold Matches under Kennel Club Regu-
lations £1.15

For permission to hold an Exemption Show £2.87

For permission to hold a Championship Obedience Show as a
Separate Event or part of a Licence Show £11.50

For permission to hold an Open Obedience Show as a Separate
Event or part of a Licence Show £5.75

For permission to hold a Limited or Sanction Obedience Show
as a separate Event or part of a Licence or Sanction Show
£2.87

For Working Trials held under Kennel Club Rules:

Championship Working Trials £11.50

Open Working Trials £5.75

Members' Working Trials £2.87

Agility Tests £2.87

For Field Trials held under Kennel Club Rules:

Two-day Meeting £5.75

One-day Meeting £3.45

VAT: All above fees are inclusive of Value Added Tax.

"VIVOMIN"

Nowadays it is possible to give a more comprehensive and balanced source of Vitamin D and the other important vitamins and minerals in a ready-made compound called Vivomin, made by Crookes Laboratories Ltd. The exact dosage, based on the weight of the dog, will be found on the packet.

IMMUNISATION

The puppy's owner should discuss with his veterinary surgeon the best method to adopt. There are several efficient methods available and the veterinary surgeon is the best person to advise.

PARVOVIRUS

Since the tenth edition of this book, a new and worrying disease has appeared which is particularly lethal to young puppies. Parvovirus made its first appearance in this country in 1978 but was known in USA and Australia before this. In the latter country there is a specific vaccine available but in this country trials are still in progress and it may be a year or more before a vaccine is on the market. Parvovirus is one of a group of viruses which include feline enteritis in cats and Mink enteritis. It causes deaths in very young puppies from heart failure and older dogs and puppies have severe enteritis and vomiting. Puppies which have had (and apparently recovered from) the disease, in its enteric form, can die later from heart failure if exposed to stress (e.g. going to a new home). The disease is especially dangerous with very young puppies "in the nest". Older puppies do respond to treatment if given in time—and it is essential, if anyone suspects this disease, to obtain immediate veterinary attention.

Although at present there is no specific vaccine, some

protection is given by injecting feline enteritis vaccine (two injections of the dead vaccine given with a fortnight in between). Some veterinary surgeons advise injecting a bitch just after mating in the hope of protecting the unborn young by maternal antibodies, but other veterinary surgeons advise against this, so you must be guided by your own veterinary surgeon. Although this a feline vaccine after-effects, from what I hear, are rare, although some dogs and puppies are a bit "loose" for a short while. I have had no reactions with my own dogs and puppies. Puppies "in the nest" can be injected if circumstances warrant this, for instance in a large kennel regularly exhibiting.

Parvovirus is an extremely contagious disease and very easily carried on shoes, clothing and, of course, on the feet and coats of dogs after shows. So the chapter on isolation after shows is very important. Anyone showing with a young litter at home runs the risk of carrying the infection back, even if their show stock have been vaccinated with feline enteritis vaccine. So strict isolation and particular attention to hygiene must be the order of the day. Veterinary surgeons differ in their attitude to this new menace and some think the danger has been greatly exaggerated. But it is prudent to take all possible precautions and the British Small Animal Veterinary Association is, I understand, very much in favour of these. Let us hope that it will not be too long before it is possible to protect our puppies as successfully against this disease as against the old horrors, hard pad, distemper, infectious hepatitis and leptospirosis!

APPENDIX

I use (and can recommend) the following, which are mentioned in this book. All drugs cited have the approval of my veterinary surgeon.

There are many excellent preparations on the market such as "Vivomin", "Vionate" and "Stress" which supply all the vitamin and mineral requirements for a healthy growing puppy.

"Collo-cal-D (Veterinary)", Iodine Oil, "Collovet", Calamine Lotion and "Vivomin" are all preparations of Crookes Laboratories, Ltd.

"Disprin" is a preparation of aspirin made by Messrs. Reckitts & Colman, who also manufacture "Dettol".

Chloretone (in capsule form) is a preparation of Messrs. Parke Davis & Co. Ltd.

Penicillin eye ointment and "Thalazole" (M. and B.)—the "sulpha" drug acting on the intestines—must be obtained from one's veterinary surgeon. The same applies to penicillin for injection and to all the sulphonamide group of drugs.

Yeast tablets: The well-known "Vetzymes" are excellent for this purpose.

Milk food: For hand-rearing, I use Humanised Truefood; for ordinary rearing, Ostermilk No. 2.

"Epivax" (and "Epivax-plus"), with several other vaccines which are prepared by tissue culture for the prophylactic and therapeutic use in distemper and "hard pad". Vaccines against leptospiral jaundice and contagious Hepatitis are also available together with, or separate from, distemper vaccine.

How to make milk food for hand-rearing puppies: Mix 3 oz. water (just off the boil) with 1 oz. milk powder. For ordinary weaning, mix 4 oz. water to 1 oz. milk powder.

Another very simple way of making baby milk food is to use Carnation Full Cream Milk diluted half and half with hot water and a little honey added. I am indebted for this tip to a well-known Sheltie breeder. I have found it excellent and far easier than mixing baby milk food.

INDEX

A

Abortion, causes and treatment of, 24
Acetylpromazine, 45
"Acid" milk, 40
Afterbirth: removal of, 37; retained, signs of, 41
Appendix, 97
Appetite, lack of: in pregnancy, 24; in "hard pad", 82
Aspirin, 88

B

Beds, whelping, 30–1
Benzyl benzoate, 73
Bismuth, 76
Bitch: age for breeding from, 18; loan of, 15; precautions in choosing, 13, 15; pregnant, diet for, 25–6; care during pregnancy, 23–5, 31–2; how to lift and carry a pregnant, 23
Bone: diet for good, 25, 54; exercise to ensure good, 62–3
Bone meal, necessity of, 25, 47–8, 54
Bones: inadvisability of, 69–70; rubber, 69
Boracic: lotion, 50, 75; powder, 43
Brandy, for moribund puppies, 47
Bread, brown, 25, 41, 53–6, 58
Breeding, 15–17; breeding terms, 13–14
Brood bitch, choice of, 13, 15
Bulldog clips for netting at shows, 93

C

Calamine Lotion (Veterinary) for ears, 76; for skin troubles, 72
Caesarian sections, 35, 36

Calcium: deficiency of, 25, 47–8; subcutaneous injection of, 48
"Canker", 76
"Carriers" (see hepatitis (viral))
Case histories, 79
Castor oil, 75, 88; and zinc ointment, 76
Chloretone: for fits, 87; before journeys, 21; after whelping, 45
Chlorodyne, 76
Clinker for runs, 60–1
Cod liver oil: fat content of, 72; necessity of, 25, 47, 54–5
Collapse, 84
"Collovet", 90
Coma, 84
Conception, prevention of, 22
Concrete for runs, 60
Constipation, 88
Cord, umbilical, 37
Cornflakes, 54–5
Cough: coughs and colds, 77; glycerine for, 77
Cysts, interdigital, 77

D

D.D.T., 71
Demodectic mange, 73
Depression in viral hepatitis, 84
Dermatitis, 71–4, 77
Dettol, 31, 35, 78
Dew-claws, removal of, 44
Diarrhoea: after whelping, 41; diet and treatment for, 75–6; possible causes of, 75–6
Difficult whelping breeds, 65
Discharge: from ears, 76; from eyes, 74–5; from nose, 79–80; from vagina, 16–19, 24–5